The Upcycled Dream

From Fabric Scraps to Fashion Week

"This book is a work of fiction. While the character of Pennelopi and her journey were inspired by the spirit and creativity of a real individual, the story, characters, and events contained within are entirely products of imagination and are not based on real life. This narrative was created with the assistance of artificial intelligence."

By Richard Dell Schwarz

Foreword

To my dear granddaughter, Pennelopi,

From the moment you arrived in this world, you brought with you a light and spirit that could never be dimmed. Watching you grow has been one of the greatest joys of my life—your curiosity, your creativity, and the quiet strength you carry with such grace remind me that the future is in very good hands.

This book is a reflection of dreams—how they begin humbly, often stitched together from scraps of hope and imagination, and how, with perseverance, they can become something beautiful and lasting. In many ways, it is also a reflection of *you.*

As you turn these pages, I hope you see a bit of yourself in the story—not only in the triumphs and the beauty, but in the challenges and doubts too. For it is through those moments that we grow the most.

Pennelopi, never stop dreaming. Never stop creating. And never forget how deeply loved and endlessly proud I am to be your granddad.

With all my heart,
Granddad

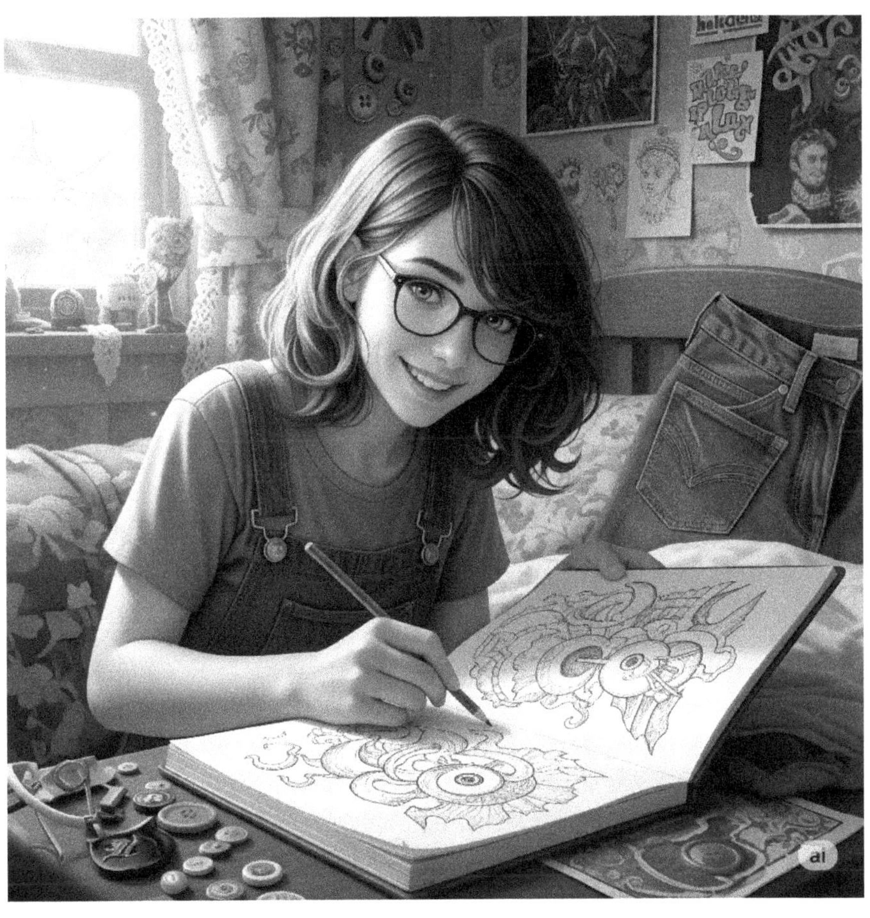

Contents

Chapter 1: Threads of Hope

The late afternoon sun, a pale, watery gold, filtered through the grimy windowpane of Pennelopi Minyen's small bedroom, illuminating dust motes dancing in the air like tiny, forgotten stars. It cast long, wavering shadows across piles of fabric that rose from the floor like miniature, colorful mountains – a landscape of discarded dreams. Pennelopi, her nose almost touching the worn pages of her sketchbook, adjusted the wire frames of her glasses, pushing them higher up the bridge of her nose. A stray strand of dark, fine hair escaped her messy bun and tickled her cheek, but she barely noticed. Her entire world, at this moment, was confined to the intricate lines and shaded forms taking shape under her pencil.

She was sketching a gown, a fantastical creation that defied the mundane reality of her life. It was a ball gown, voluminous and ethereal, made not of silk or satin, but of meticulously layered strips of faded denim, each edge frayed just so, creating a soft, textural cascade. The bodice, she imagined, would be a mosaic of antique lace doilies, dyed in subtle ombré shades of indigo and cream, painstakingly stitched together to form a delicate, almost sculptural armor. Tiny, mismatched buttons, scavenged from countless forgotten garments, would serve as glittering embellishments, catching the light like scattered jewels. On the page, it was magnificent, a silent testament to the vibrant, restless imagination that churned beneath Pennelopi's quiet exterior.

Pennelopi Minyen was, by all accounts, a girl who blended into the background. Her glasses, thick-rimmed and perpetually smudged, often hid eyes that were surprisingly intense and observant, the color of deep moss after a rain. Her posture was habitually hunched, a defensive curl that seemed to protect the vast, intricate world she carried within. In school, she spoke only when directly addressed, her voice a soft murmur that often got lost in the boisterous symphony of teenage chatter. She preferred the company of books and her own thoughts, finding solace in the predictable narratives of fiction and the silent, accepting presence of her fabrics. This shyness wasn't a choice; it was an innate part of her, a pervasive fog that seemed to cling to her, making every social interaction feel like navigating a dense, unfamiliar forest. Even ordering a coffee at the local diner could induce a flush that crept up her neck and burned her ears.

But here, in her room, surrounded by the tangible evidence of her passion, the shyness evaporated.

Here, she was bold. Here, her voice, though unspoken, roared. The fabrics were her language, the needle and thread her eloquent prose. She wasn't just making clothes; she was telling stories, breathing new life into forgotten textiles, whispering secrets of sustainability and beauty into every stitch.

Her family's financial struggles were a constant, low hum beneath the surface of their lives, a subtle but pervasive pressure that shaped every decision. It wasn't a dramatic, sudden poverty, but a slow, grinding attrition. Her father worked long hours at a manufacturing plant, his hands permanently stained with grease, his shoulders perpetually slumped with fatigue. Her mother juggled two part-time jobs – cleaning offices in the early mornings and working as a cashier at a discount grocery store in the evenings – her smile, though ever-present, often seemed stretched thin. There were no lavish vacations, no brand-new clothes, no expensive gadgets. Every penny was accounted for, every purchase considered, every indulgence a luxury they simply couldn't afford.

Pennelopi understood this reality with a quiet maturity beyond her years. She saw the worry lines etched deeper around her parents' eyes, the way they sometimes spoke in hushed tones after she and her younger brother, Leo, had gone to bed. She knew why her school textbooks were always hand-me-downs, why her sneakers had holes in the soles, why the family car coughed and sputtered with alarming regularity. This understanding, while heavy, also fueled her creativity. It was precisely *because* she couldn't afford expensive materials or trendy outfits that she had discovered the boundless potential of the discarded.

Her journey into upcycling had begun innocently enough, born out of necessity. When she was twelve, she'd desperately wanted a new dress for the school dance, something unique, something that wasn't from the same fast-fashion chain everyone else wore. Her mother, with a sigh of regret, had gently explained that it wasn't in the budget. Disappointed but not defeated, Pennelopi had wandered into a local thrift store, drawn by the chaotic jumble of forgotten garments. There, amidst the racks of ill-fitting sweaters and stained t-shirts, she'd found it: a voluminous, floral-patterned curtain, its fabric faded in places, but still vibrant in others. An idea, a spark, had ignited. She'd bought it for a dollar, dragged it home, and, with her mother's old, clunky sewing machine and a YouTube tutorial, she'd transformed it into a surprisingly chic, high-waisted skirt. It wasn't perfect, but it was *hers*, and it was beautiful. The feeling of accomplishment, the thrill of creation from nothing, had been intoxicating. From that day on, the thrift store became her treasure trove, the discarded her canvas.

Now, her room was a testament to this obsession. The air itself seemed to carry the faint, mingled scent of old cotton, laundered wool, and the metallic tang of her sewing machine. Her desk, a chipped hand-me-down from her grandmother, was perpetually buried under spools of thread, fabric scissors, measuring tapes, and a collection of vintage buttons she'd meticulously sorted by color and size into old glass jars. A mannequin, a headless, armless torso she'd found abandoned on the curb outside a defunct boutique, stood sentinel in the corner, draped in a half-finished garment – a jacket crafted from an old army surplus blanket, its rough texture softened by panels of delicate, embroidered handkerchiefs.

The process of upcycling was almost a ritual for Pennelopi. It began with the hunt. Every Saturday, if she could convince her dad to drop her off, she'd spend hours at the local Goodwill or Salvation Army, her keen eyes scanning the racks, not for what something *was*, but for what it *could be*. A men's XXL flannel shirt wasn't just a shirt; it was potential for a deconstructed skirt or a patchwork vest. A moth-eaten cashmere sweater wasn't trash; it was luxurious yarn for embellishments or a soft lining. She'd run her fingers over fabrics, feeling their weight, their drape, their history. She'd hold them up to the light, imagining how they would transform. Sometimes, she'd come home empty-handed, but more often, she'd emerge victorious, clutching a bag filled with what others considered junk, but what she saw as raw, precious material.

Then came the deconstruction. This was a meticulous, almost surgical phase. With a small seam ripper, she'd carefully unpick stitches, liberating fabric panels from their original forms. It was a meditative process, each snip of thread a small act of liberation. She learned about garment construction this way, understanding how a sleeve was set, how a collar was shaped, how seams were finished. She saw the bones of clothing, the underlying architecture, which in turn informed her own designs. She'd wash and press every piece of salvaged fabric, sometimes dyeing them with natural pigments she extracted from onion skins or avocado pits, giving them a new, vibrant life.

The reassembly was where the magic truly happened. Pennelopi didn't just patch things together; she sculpted. She draped, she folded, she layered. She experimented with textures, juxtaposing rough denim with delicate lace, sturdy canvas with flowing silk. Her designs were often asymmetrical, playful, and deeply personal. She wasn't chasing trends; she was creating art. Her sewing machine, a vintage Singer, hummed a steady, comforting lullaby as she fed fabric through its needle, transforming flat pieces into three-dimensional forms. Sometimes, she'd work late into the night, the only sound the rhythmic whir of the machine and the occasional snip of her scissors, lost in the quiet ecstasy of creation.

The burden of her shyness, however, remained a heavy cloak she wore outside her room. It wasn't just a lack of confidence; it was a physical sensation, a tightening in her chest, a prickle of heat on her skin whenever she felt eyes on her. In class, she knew the answers to questions, but the thought of raising her hand, of speaking aloud, was paralyzing. She'd rehearse conversations in her head, perfect witty remarks or insightful observations, only to have them dissolve into awkward silence when the moment arrived. She envied the effortless confidence of her peers, the way they laughed loudly, shared opinions freely, and moved through the world with an unburdened ease. She often wondered if her passion for fashion was just another way to hide, to let her creations speak for her because she couldn't speak for herself.

Her dreams, however, were anything but shy. In the secret corners of her mind, Pennelopi envisioned herself on grand stages, her designs parading down runways under dazzling lights. She saw herself, not just as a creator, but as a voice, advocating for sustainable fashion, proving that beauty didn't have to come at the expense of the planet or people. New York Fashion Week, a distant, shimmering mirage, was the ultimate destination in these nocturnal fantasies. It felt utterly impossible, a fantasy too grand for a girl who struggled to make eye contact with the grocery store cashier.

One particularly frustrating afternoon, after a grueling day at school where she'd stumbled over her words during a simple presentation, Pennelopi retreated to her room, feeling the familiar sting of self-reproach. She threw her backpack onto the floor, the thud echoing in the quiet space. Her eyes landed on the half-finished denim-and-lace gown from her sketch. It looked so vibrant on paper, so full of life. But translating it into reality, with her limited resources and even more limited social courage, felt like trying to catch smoke.

She picked up a scrap of faded floral fabric, a remnant from an old sundress, and ran it through her fingers. It was soft, worn smooth by countless washes, carrying the faint scent of laundry detergent and memories not her own. This fabric, once loved, then discarded, now held the promise of something new. It was a metaphor for herself, she realized. Faded, overlooked, but with the potential for transformation.

A sudden gust of wind rattled the windowpane, and a small, brightly colored flyer, previously unnoticed, fluttered from beneath a pile of magazines on her desk. It was printed on recycled paper, its vibrant green and blue hues catching her eye. Pennelopi picked it up, her brow furrowing slightly.

"Green Stitch" Upcycled Fashion Show, the bold headline read. "Celebrate creativity, sustainability, and community!" Below it, details about entry requirements, categories, and judging criteria. A local event. A community art fair. A chance to showcase unique designs.

Pennelopi's breath hitched. Her heart, which usually beat with a quiet, steady rhythm, began to thrum against her ribs like a trapped bird. This wasn't New York Fashion Week, not even close. But it was a runway. A real one. In her own town.

A wave of conflicting emotions washed over her. Excitement, sharp and exhilarating, mixed with a familiar, suffocating dread. The thought of her designs, her secret passion, being seen by others, judged by others, filled her with a thrilling terror. And then there was the inevitable part: talking about her work, explaining her vision, standing in front of people. Her palms grew sweaty just thinking about it.

She reread the flyer, her eyes darting over the words. "Showcase your unique designs." "Skepticism and competition from more privileged teens." The words seemed to jump off the page, mirroring her deepest fears. She imagined the other contestants, confident and polished, their creations made from expensive, pristine fabrics. Would her upcycled pieces look cheap, amateurish, next to theirs? Would they laugh at her?

A small, insistent voice in her head, however, pushed back. *But what if they don't? What if they see what you see?*

She traced the outline of the denim-and-lace gown in her sketchbook. It was a bold design, a statement. It was a piece that demanded attention. Could she, Pennelopi, the girl who hid behind her glasses and her hair, truly create something that demanded attention?

Just then, a knock on her bedroom door. "Pennelopi? You in there?" It was Liam, her best friend, his voice muffled through the wood.

Liam was the antithesis of Pennelopi. He was outgoing, boisterous, and possessed an infectious enthusiasm for life. He was also an aspiring photographer, always with a camera slung around his neck, constantly seeing the world through a lens, capturing its beauty and its imperfections. He was one of the very few people with whom Pennelopi felt completely at ease, someone who saw past her shyness to the vibrant creativity within. He was her anchor, her loudest cheerleader, and her most patient listener.

"Yeah, come in," Pennelopi called out, her voice still a little tight from her internal turmoil.

The door creaked open, and Liam's head, topped with a perpetually tousled mop of brown hair, poked through. His eyes, bright and curious, immediately swept over the organized chaos of her room. "Whoa, new fabric mountains? What's the latest masterpiece brewing?" He stepped inside, his camera bag thudding softly as he set it down.

Pennelopi hesitated, then held out the flyer. "Look what I found."

Liam took it, his eyes scanning the text. His face lit up. "The 'Green Stitch' show! No way! Pennelopi, this is perfect for you!" He looked at her, his excitement palpable. "You *have* to enter. Your stuff is incredible. Seriously, you make magic out of old rags."

Pennelopi's cheeks flushed. "I don't know, Liam. It's… a show. People will be there. And judging." She gestured vaguely towards her piles of fabric. "And it's all upcycled. What if it looks… less than?"

Liam scoffed, waving a dismissive hand. "Less than? Are you kidding? That's the whole point! 'Upcycled Fashion Show,' Pennelopi. Your designs are exactly what they're looking for. And who cares what anyone else thinks? Your art speaks for itself. And besides," he grinned, "I need some amazing subjects for my portfolio. Imagine the shots I could get of your pieces on a real runway!"

His enthusiasm was infectious, a warm current that began to chip away at Pennelopi's icy dread. Liam had always believed in her, even when she didn't believe in herself. He was the one who had first encouraged her to take her sketching seriously, who had convinced her to start posting blurry photos of her finished pieces on a private Instagram account, just for them. He saw the potential, the artistry, where she only saw her own limitations.

"But… talking," Pennelopi mumbled, her voice barely a whisper. "I'd have to… explain things. To judges. To people." The thought alone made her stomach churn.

Liam's smile softened. He knew her shyness, respected it, but also gently pushed against it. "You don't have to give a TED Talk, Pen. Just be yourself. Let your clothes do most of the talking. And I'll be there, front row, cheering you on. We can practice what you'll say. You'll be great." He picked up her sketchbook, flipping through the pages. "This gown, for example," he said, his voice full of genuine admiration. "It's stunning. The way you've used the denim, it's like a story. You just tell them the story of the fabric, the story of your vision. It's not about being loud; it's about being true."

Pennelopi looked at the flyer again, then at her sketchbook, then at the half-finished jacket on the mannequin. The idea, once terrifying, now sparked a flicker of hope. It was a tiny, fragile flame, but it was there. This wasn't just about a fashion show; it was about stepping out of the shadows, about letting her art, and perhaps even a small part of herself, finally be seen. It was a daunting prospect, but the thought of *not* trying, of letting this opportunity slip away, felt even worse. The upcycled dream, she realized, was not just about transforming fabric; it was about transforming herself. The first thread, she knew, had just been pulled.

Chapter 2: The Community Canvas

The door clicked shut behind Liam, leaving Pennelopi in the sudden, amplified silence of her bedroom. The faint scent of old cotton and the metallic tang of her sewing machine seemed to cling to the air, comforting in their familiarity. But the quiet was no longer peaceful. It hummed with a new, insistent energy, vibrating with the unspoken challenge of the flyer clutched in her hand.

"Green Stitch" Upcycled Fashion Show. The words, once a distant, almost abstract concept, now pulsed with a terrifying immediacy. Liam's boundless enthusiasm, his unwavering belief in her, had momentarily swept away the suffocating fog of her shyness. But now, alone, the fog began to creep back in, tendrils of doubt curling around her nascent hope.

She walked slowly to her desk, the recycled paper crinkling softly in her grip. She laid it flat, smoothing out the creases, as if the act of flattening the paper could flatten the tumultuous emotions swirling within her. Her eyes scanned the details again: "Open to all local artists and designers," "Emphasis on sustainable materials," "Judging based on creativity, craftsmanship, and thematic interpretation." And then, the part that made her stomach clench: "Presentations will be required for finalists."

Presentations. The word hung in the air, heavy and suffocating. Pennelopi's mind immediately conjured images of past failures: the trembling voice during a book report in middle school, the flushed cheeks and stammered apologies when asked to explain a math problem on the board, the way her carefully rehearsed lines for a drama club audition had dissolved into an unintelligible mumble. Her shyness wasn't just a quiet demeanor; it was a physical barrier, a wall that rose up, solid and impenetrable, whenever she was placed under the spotlight. Her throat would constrict, her heart would hammer a frantic rhythm against her ribs, and her mind, usually so sharp and imaginative, would go utterly blank. It was a cruel irony that her hands, so capable and expressive with fabric, belonged to a body that froze in social situations.

She sighed, a long, shaky exhale that did little to dispel the tension. It wasn't just the fear of public speaking. It was the fear of exposure. Her upcycled creations were more than just clothes; they were fragments of her soul, stitched together with hours of quiet dedication and infused with her deepest convictions about beauty, sustainability, and finding value in the overlooked. To put them out there, to have them scrutinized, to have *her* scrutinized, felt like stripping herself bare. What if they didn't understand? What if they saw only the "old rags" Liam so affectionately referred to, and not the stories, the transformations, the art?

And then there was the financial aspect, a constant, low thrum beneath the surface of all their lives. Her parents worked tirelessly, their bodies aching, their spirits sometimes weary, to keep their heads above water. Every dollar was stretched, every expense weighed. Entering this show, even a local one, would require time and, inevitably, some small investment. While her materials were salvaged, there would be threads, needles, perhaps a new zipper or button if a design absolutely demanded it. More importantly, it would consume her free time, time she sometimes spent helping her mother with chores or looking after Leo. Was pursuing this dream, this deeply personal artistic endeavor, a selfish indulgence when their family was always struggling? The thought gnawed at her, a familiar companion to her shyness. She felt a profound sense of responsibility, a silent pressure to not add to their burdens, to not waste resources on something that might ultimately lead to disappointment.

She walked over to her mannequin, the headless form draped in the half-finished army blanket jacket, now adorned with intricate panels of embroidered handkerchiefs. She ran her fingers over the rough wool, then the delicate, almost translucent cotton. The contrast was striking, a testament to her vision. This piece, like all her others, was a conversation between disparate elements, a harmony forged from discord. It was beautiful, she knew it was. But knowing it in the quiet sanctity of her room was one thing; believing it under the harsh glare of public judgment was another entirely.

The next few days were a blur of internal debate. The flyer lay on her desk, a silent challenge. She'd pick it up, read it, put it down. She'd sketch new ideas, then crumple the paper in frustration. She'd start to deconstruct an old dress, then abandon it, her mind too consumed by the "what ifs."

Liam, sensing her turmoil, became a constant, gentle presence. He didn't badger her, didn't demand a decision. Instead, he'd just *be* there. He'd bring over his camera, clicking away at her fabric piles, capturing the textures and colors, showing her the beauty she sometimes overlooked in her own creative chaos. He'd sit on her floor, cross-legged, while she worked, offering quiet observations.

"You know," he'd say one afternoon, watching her meticulously unpick a seam on a vintage tablecloth, "the light in here is amazing right now. Perfect for capturing the way that lace catches the sun." He wasn't talking about the show, not directly, but his words were a subtle reminder of the inherent beauty in her work, the beauty he saw so clearly.

Another time, he brought over a stack of fashion magazines he'd found at a garage sale – old issues, but still filled with glossy images of runway shows and designer profiles. He knew she couldn't afford new ones. "Look at this," he'd point to a avant-garde design, "they're doing something similar with layering, but yours is way more interesting because of the story behind the fabric." He was subtly validating her artistic choices, showing her that her "limitations" were actually her strengths.

"It's just… everyone else will have new stuff," Pennelopi finally confessed one evening, her voice barely audible, as she sat hunched over her sewing machine, a half-finished garment limp in her lap. "Expensive fabrics. Perfect seams. Mine will be… patched."

Liam put down his camera. "Pennelopi, that's the *point* of upcycling. It's not about perfection; it's about transformation. It's about showing that beauty isn't just about what's new and shiny. It's about ingenuity. It's about giving things a second life. That's a powerful message, way more powerful than just another pretty dress from a department store." He paused, then added, "And honestly, your seams *are* perfect. You're a meticulous freak, you know that?" He nudged her playfully, and a small, reluctant smile touched Pennelopi's lips.

He then shifted his approach, moving from reassurance to practical planning. "Okay, so let's say you *do* it. What would you need? What kind of pieces would you make? Do you have a theme in mind?" He pulled out a small notebook from his camera bag, ready to jot down ideas.

Pennelopi looked at him, surprised. "A theme?"

"Yeah, like, a narrative. Every collection tells a story, right? What story do you want to tell with your upcycled pieces?"

The question resonated deeply within Pennelopi. Her designs had always told stories, even if only to herself. The denim gown was about resilience, the lace bodice about delicate strength. The army blanket jacket was about finding softness in harshness. Liam's question reframed the challenge, turning it from a public performance into an artistic statement.

"I… I guess it's about finding beauty in what's overlooked," she mused, her gaze drifting to the piles of fabric. "About how everything has potential, even when it seems broken or discarded. And about how creativity can overcome… limits." She thought of her family, their struggles, and how she found her own way to create despite their financial constraints. "The Upcycled Dream," she whispered, the title of her dream collection forming on her lips.

Liam's eyes lit up. "Yes! That's it! 'The Upcycled Dream.' That's a killer theme, Pen! It's personal, it's powerful, and it fits the show perfectly. See? You've got this." He started scribbling furiously in his notebook. "Okay, so for the presentation, you just talk about that. About your philosophy. About the journey of the fabric. You don't have to be a stand-up comedian. Just be you, talking about what you love."

His practical approach, combined with his unwavering belief, began to chip away at her resistance. The idea of the "Green Stitch" show started to feel less like an insurmountable mountain and more like a challenging but achievable climb.

The "Green Stitch" Upcycled Fashion Show wasn't just a local event; it was a cornerstone of the community's burgeoning sustainability movement.

Held annually in the town's old, repurposed textile mill – now a vibrant community arts center – it drew a diverse crowd. Local artists, environmental activists, families looking for a unique weekend outing, and even a few curious fashion enthusiasts from the nearest city would gather. The air during the fair was always buzzing with a convivial energy, a mix of earthy idealism and creative ingenuity. There were stalls selling handmade soaps, repurposed furniture, organic produce, and, of course, the main event: the fashion show.

The runway itself was modest, a temporary stage erected in the mill's cavernous main hall, but the atmosphere was electric. String lights crisscrossed the high ceilings, casting a warm glow on the exposed brick walls. Local musicians played folk music, and the scent of homemade kombucha mingled with the faint, pleasant aroma of natural dyes. It was a place where creativity was celebrated, where the unconventional was embraced. This wasn't the cutthroat world of high fashion Pennelopi sometimes dreamed of, but it was a genuine, supportive platform, a place where her unique approach might truly be appreciated.

One evening, after a particularly long and quiet dinner, Pennelopi found herself staring at the flyer again. Her parents were in the living room, the low murmur of the television a familiar backdrop. Leo was already asleep. The house was quiet, save for the distant hum of the refrigerator. She thought about Liam's words, about "The Upcycled Dream." She thought about the denim gown, the army blanket jacket, the countless other designs swirling in her head. She thought about the feeling of the fabric under her fingers, the quiet satisfaction of a perfectly straight seam, the thrill of seeing a discarded item transform into something beautiful.

And then, a memory surfaced. Not a grand, pivotal moment, but a small, quiet one. A few weeks ago, her mother had been about to throw away an old, faded tablecloth, stained in places, but with a beautiful, intricate floral embroidery along the edges. Pennelopi had stopped her, rescued it, and later, without a word, had incorporated a section of the embroidery into the cuff of a simple, upcycled blouse she'd made for herself. The next morning, her mother had noticed it. She hadn't said much, just a small, surprised smile and a gentle touch to the embroidered cuff. In that moment, Pennelopi had felt a warmth spread through her, a quiet validation that transcended words. It wasn't about money or prestige; it was about seeing value, about creating beauty, about making something out of nothing.

That small, silent moment was the push she needed. If she could bring that quiet joy to her mother, perhaps she could bring it to others. Perhaps her art *could* speak for her.

She took a deep breath, pulled out her phone, and found the email address listed on the flyer. Her fingers hovered over the keyboard, hesitating. Then, with a surge of determination that surprised even herself, she typed out a brief, formal email expressing her interest in entering the "Green Stitch" Upcycled Fashion Show, outlining her theme, "The Upcycled Dream," and attaching a few photos Liam had taken of her existing pieces. She hit send before she could second-guess herself.

The moment the email was sent, a strange mix of exhilaration and terror washed over her. It was done. The first step was taken. There was no turning back.

The next morning, she told her parents. She approached them cautiously at the breakfast table, where her father was already nursing a mug of coffee and her mother was packing Leo's lunch.

"Um, Mom, Dad," Pennelopi began, her voice a little shaky. "I… I signed up for something."

Her father looked up, his brow furrowed slightly. "Signed up for what, honey?"

"It's a… a fashion show. A local one. For upcycled clothes." She quickly explained the concept, the "Green Stitch" event, and her theme. She watched their faces, bracing herself for their reaction.

Her mother paused, a sandwich half-wrapped in her hand. "A fashion show? Pennelopi, that's… that's wonderful! But, honey, you know we don't have much for… for fancy materials."

"No, that's the thing," Pennelopi explained, her voice gaining a little more confidence as she spoke about her passion. "It's all about using old clothes, discarded fabrics. It's what I already do. And Liam said he could help me with photos for the submission, and he's excited about taking pictures at the show."

Her father put down his coffee mug. He looked at her, really looked at her, his usual tired expression softening into something akin to curiosity, then pride. "So, all those hours you spend with your sewing machine, that's for this? This 'upcycled' thing?"

Pennelopi nodded, feeling a blush creep up her neck. "Yeah. It's… it's my dream, Dad. To be a designer. And this is a chance to show what I can do."

Her mother came over and gently squeezed her shoulder. "Well, if it makes you happy, darling. We'll support you however we can. Just… don't overdo it, okay? School's important too." There was a hint of worry in her eyes, but also a genuine warmth. They might not fully grasp the world of fashion design, but they understood her passion, and that was enough.

Leo, who had been quietly eating his cereal, piped up, "Are you gonna make me a superhero cape out of old towels?"

Pennelopi laughed, a genuine, unburdened sound. "Maybe, Leo. Maybe." Her brother's innocent question, her parents' cautious but undeniable support, filled her with a renewed sense of purpose. She wasn't just doing this for herself; she was doing it for them, too. To show them that her "hobby" had real value, that her dreams, however unconventional, were worth pursuing.

With the decision made, a new energy surged through Pennelopi. Her room, once a sanctuary for private creation, now transformed into a vibrant workshop for public display. The creative process for the "Green Stitch" collection began with a feverish intensity.

She started by sketching. Not just individual garments, but an entire cohesive collection that embodied "The Upcycled Dream." She wanted to tell a story of transformation, of evolution. Her initial ideas revolved around three distinct looks, each showcasing a different facet of upcycling and a different mood.

The first look, she decided, would be her most ambitious: a deconstructed formal gown, a direct descendant of the denim-and-lace sketch. She envisioned it as a "phoenix dress," rising from the ashes of discarded everyday wear. For this, she needed a vast array of denim scraps, not just from jeans, but from jackets, skirts, even old denim bags. She wanted varying shades of blue, from deep indigo to bleached-out sky, to create a gradient effect. The lace elements would come from vintage tablecloths, curtains, and even delicate lingerie found at estate sales – pieces that whispered of forgotten elegance. The challenge would be to make the denim, a typically heavy and casual fabric, flow and drape with the ethereal quality of a ball gown. She spent hours meticulously cutting denim strips, fraying edges by hand, and experimenting with different layering techniques on her mannequin. The lace, once unpicked, was carefully washed and sometimes dyed in subtle tea stains or diluted indigo baths to give it an aged, cohesive look.

The second look would be more avant-garde, a statement piece that truly pushed the boundaries of upcycling. She called it "Urban Bloom." This would be a sculptural jacket and skirt ensemble, crafted primarily from repurposed canvas – old tarps, army surplus bags, even worn-out tents. The stiffness of the canvas would allow for dramatic, architectural shapes. To soften and juxtapose this utilitarian base, she planned to incorporate bursts of vibrant, unexpected color and texture: patches of silk scarves, embroidered remnants from old kimonos, and even deconstructed floral patterns cut from vintage dresses. The "bloom" would come from three-dimensional fabric flowers, meticulously hand-stitched from various scraps, bursting forth from the canvas, symbolizing nature reclaiming the urban landscape. This piece was a direct challenge to her own meticulous nature; it required a looser, more experimental approach, allowing the materials to guide the form.

For the third and final look, Pennelopi wanted something more wearable, something that showcased the everyday elegance possible with upcycling. This would be "Comfort Reimagined," a sophisticated loungewear set. She envisioned a flowing tunic and wide-leg trousers made from a patchwork of soft, luxurious knits: cashmere sweaters, merino wool scarves, and even silk pajama bottoms, all carefully selected for their drape and texture. The challenge here would be to create a seamless, cohesive look from such disparate materials, focusing on subtle color palettes and the inherent comfort of the fabrics. Buttons from old cardigans, delicate embroidery from forgotten linens, and even small, hand-stitched details would elevate the loungewear from casual to chic.

The hunt for materials intensified. Her Saturday trips to the thrift store became strategic expeditions. She developed an almost uncanny ability to spot potential amidst the clutter. She learned to recognize the quality of a fabric by touch, to estimate how much usable material she could salvage from a garment, to see the hidden beauty in a faded print or a slightly torn hem. She wasn't just buying clothes; she was acquiring raw materials, each piece a puzzle waiting to be solved.

One memorable Saturday, she stumbled upon a treasure trove: a box of old, hand-embroidered handkerchiefs, forgotten in a dusty corner of the Goodwill. They were delicate, some with tiny monograms, others with intricate floral patterns, all whispering of a bygone era. These, she knew instantly, would be perfect for the "Urban Bloom" jacket, adding a touch of fragile beauty to the rugged canvas. Another time, she found a stack of perfectly preserved, albeit faded, denim jackets, their varying washes offering the exact gradient she needed for the "phoenix dress." Each find was a small victory, a confirmation that her vision was achievable, piece by precious piece.

The deconstruction phase became a meditative ritual, a quiet conversation with the fabric. She'd lay out a garment, studying its construction, imagining its past life. With her seam ripper, she'd carefully unpick stitches, liberating panels of fabric. It was a slow, deliberate process, sometimes tedious, but always rewarding. She learned the anatomy of clothing, the hidden logic of seams and darts. She learned patience. She learned that even something seemingly whole could be broken down, reimagined, and rebuilt into something entirely new and stronger. She'd wash and press each salvaged piece, sometimes dyeing them in her backyard with natural pigments – onion skins for a subtle gold, avocado pits for a dusty rose, black beans for a deep indigo – transforming their original hues into a cohesive palette for her collection.

The reassembly was where the true artistry unfolded. Pennelopi worked with a focused intensity, her brow furrowed in concentration, her fingers flying over the fabric. The vintage Singer sewing machine, a gift from her grandmother, hummed a steady, comforting rhythm, a mechanical heartbeat in her quiet room. She draped the denim strips onto her mannequin, experimenting with the flow, the way the frayed edges caught the light. She meticulously stitched the lace doilies together, creating a delicate, almost three-dimensional texture for the bodice of the phoenix dress. For the "Urban Bloom" jacket, she wrestled with the stiff canvas, cutting and shaping it into sharp, architectural forms, then carefully hand-stitching the vibrant silk and embroidered patches, making the fabric flowers bloom from the utilitarian base. The "Comfort Reimagined" set required a different kind of precision, blending the varied textures and weights of the knits into a seamless, luxurious whole.

There were challenges, of course. The denim, being heavy, resisted her attempts to make it drape elegantly. She experimented with different cutting techniques, bias cuts, and even subtle pleating to achieve the desired fluidity. The canvas, while holding its shape well, was difficult to sew through in multiple layers, testing the limits of her old Singer.

She learned to reinforce seams, to use stronger needles, and to take breaks when her fingers ached. There were moments of frustration, when a seam wouldn't lie flat, or a fabric wouldn't behave as she intended. In those moments, she'd step away, take a deep breath, and return with fresh eyes, often finding an ingenious solution that transformed the problem into a unique design element. A stubborn wrinkle might become a deliberate fold, a frayed edge a purposeful detail.

Her family, initially cautious, slowly became accustomed to the sight of Pennelopi surrounded by fabric scraps, her room a perpetual state of organized chaos. Her mother would sometimes peek in, offering a cup of tea or a plate of cookies, her eyes lingering on the evolving garments with a quiet pride. "That's looking beautiful, honey," she'd say, her voice soft, a rare compliment that meant the world to Pennelopi.

Her father, usually reserved, would occasionally stop by her door on his way to work, his gaze sweeping over her creations. "You know, that jacket reminds me of the old canvas tarp we used for camping," he remarked one morning, pointing to the "Urban Bloom" piece. "Never thought it could look like that." It was his way of acknowledging her skill, of seeing the transformation she wrought.

Leo, her younger brother, was a source of endless, innocent amusement. He'd wander into her room, his eyes wide with curiosity, and ask questions that were both insightful and utterly childlike. "Why are you cutting up that old blanket, Pennelopi? Isn't it cold?" or "Can I have the shiny buttons when you're done?" He often tried to "help" by sorting her fabric scraps into bizarre, illogical piles, or by attempting to draw on her designs with crayons, leading to a few near-disasters and much laughter. But his presence, his uncritical acceptance of her strange, fabric-filled world, was a comfort. He saw her as "Pennelopi who makes cool clothes," not "Pennelopi who's shy."

Liam, true to his word, was her constant co-conspirator. He'd come over almost daily after school, not just to offer moral support, but to actively help. He'd hold fabrics for her while she pinned, help her organize her ever-growing collection of salvaged materials, and even, to her surprise, proved quite adept at unpicking seams, his long fingers surprisingly nimble.

"Okay, Pen," he announced one afternoon, after she'd successfully completed the "phoenix dress," its denim layers cascading beautifully on the mannequin. "Time for presentation practice."

Pennelopi groaned, her shoulders slumping. "Do we have to? It's still weeks away."

"Yes, we have to," Liam insisted, pulling out his phone. "I'm going to record you. Think of it as a dress rehearsal for your voice. You're going to stand here, in front of the mannequin, and explain your piece. Pretend I'm the judge."

Pennelopi's heart began to pound. Her palms grew clammy. "But… what do I say?"

"Start with your theme. 'The Upcycled Dream.' Then talk about this dress. Where did the materials come from? What was your inspiration? What challenges did you face? How did you overcome them? What message do you want to convey?" Liam coached her patiently, breaking it down into manageable chunks.

Her first attempts were disastrous. Her voice was a barely audible whisper, her eyes fixed on the floor. She stammered, lost her train of thought, and often resorted to pointing vaguely at the dress. Liam would stop the recording, offering gentle corrections.

"Speak up, Pen. Imagine you're talking to someone across the room. Look at me, not the floor. You know this stuff inside out. Just tell me about it like you're telling me about a new book you read."

Slowly, painstakingly, Pennelopi began to improve. She started by focusing on the fabric itself, describing its journey from discarded item to artistic material. She talked about the texture of the denim, the history of the lace, the painstaking process of deconstruction and reassembly. As she spoke about the tangible elements, the physical act of creation, her voice gained strength. She found that when she focused on the *art*, the fear of the *audience* receded, if only slightly.

"This denim," she explained one evening, her voice still soft but clearer, "it came from about ten different pairs of jeans. Each one had its own story, its own wear patterns. I wanted to bring those stories together, to show how something so ordinary could become extraordinary." She gestured to the bodice. "And the lace… these were old doilies, some stained, some torn. I repaired them, dyed them, and then stitched them together to create this mosaic. It's about finding beauty in imperfection, about mending what's broken."

Liam watched her, a proud smile on his face. "See? That's it! That's powerful, Pen. You're not just making a dress; you're telling a philosophy. Keep practicing that. You've got a great story to tell."

The weeks leading up to the submission deadline were a whirlwind of creation and quiet anticipation. Pennelopi spent every spare moment in her room, surrounded by her fabric mountains, the rhythmic hum of her sewing machine a constant companion. The phoenix dress took shape, its denim layers rippling like water, the lace bodice a delicate masterpiece. The "Urban Bloom" jacket grew bolder with each stitched-on flower and vibrant patch, a striking contrast of ruggedness and beauty. The "Comfort Reimagined" loungewear became a tactile symphony of soft knits, a testament to subtle luxury born from humble beginnings.

As each piece neared completion, Pennelopi felt a nascent sense of confidence bloom within her. It wasn't a sudden, dramatic transformation, but a slow, steady growth, like a seed pushing through the soil. She was still Pennelopi, the girl with the glasses and the quiet voice, but something fundamental had shifted. She was building something, creating something tangible and beautiful, and in doing so, she was building herself.

The day of the submission arrived. Pennelopi, with Liam by her side, carefully packed her three finished garments into large, repurposed garment bags. Her heart pounded with a mix of excitement and sheer terror. This was it. The culmination of weeks of intense work, of overcoming her doubts, of daring to dream.

As they walked to the community arts center, Liam carried the heaviest bag, his camera slung over his shoulder. "Remember what we practiced," he reminded her, his voice calm and reassuring. "Deep breaths. Talk about the fabric. Talk about the dream."

Pennelopi nodded, her throat tight. The air was crisp, the sky a brilliant, hopeful blue. She looked at the bags, at the shapes of her creations within them. They were more than just clothes. They were her voice, finally ready to be heard. The "Green Stitch" show wasn't just a competition; it was a canvas, a chance for her upcycled dream to finally take flight. The first thread had been pulled, and now, the tapestry was beginning to unfold.

Chapter 3: The Skeptic's Eye

The community arts center, an old textile mill repurposed with a hopeful vision, loomed before Pennelopi and Liam like a colossal, brick-built beast. Its windows, once grimy and dark, now gleamed faintly in the morning sun, reflecting the crisp, hopeful blue of the sky. A large banner, emblazoned with the "Green Stitch" logo – a stylized needle threading a leaf – fluttered gently above the main entrance, announcing the annual Upcycled Fashion Show and community fair. Despite the cheerful banner, Pennelopi's stomach churned with a nervous energy that felt entirely at odds with the gentle breeze.

"This is it," Liam said, his voice a low, encouraging rumble beside her. He adjusted the strap of the heavy garment bag slung over his shoulder, which contained Pennelopi's "phoenix dress." Pennelopi clutched her own bag, containing the "Urban Bloom" jacket and "Comfort Reimagined" loungewear, so tightly her knuckles were white. The fabric within, usually a source of comfort and pride, now felt vulnerable, exposed.

They pushed through the heavy wooden doors, and the outside world, with its crisp air and gentle sunlight, instantly receded. The interior of the mill was a symphony of sounds and smells. The vast main hall, with its high ceilings and exposed brick, echoed with the cheerful chatter of early arrivals, the clinking of ceramic mugs from a pop-up coffee stand, and the distant, melodic strumming of an acoustic guitar. The air was a rich tapestry of scents: freshly brewed coffee, earthy patchouli from a nearby artisan stall, and the faint, almost nostalgic aroma of old wood and textiles.

Pennelopi's eyes darted around, taking in the scene. The space was already bustling. Volunteers in bright green t-shirts moved purposefully, setting up display tables and guiding participants. Other contestants, most of them older teens or young adults, were already present, some meticulously arranging their creations on mannequins, others chatting animatedly with friends. They exuded a casual confidence that Pennelopi could only dream of. Their clothes, even their casual attire, seemed effortlessly stylish, a stark contrast to Pennelopi's own worn jeans and oversized thrift-store sweater. She felt a familiar prickle of heat on her cheeks, a sudden urge to turn and flee.

"Deep breaths, Pen," Liam murmured, sensing her rising anxiety. He gently steered her towards the registration table, a makeshift setup near the main entrance. "Remember, you've got this. Your pieces are amazing."

At the table, a cheerful woman with bright, kind eyes greeted them. "Welcome to Green Stitch! Are you here to submit for the fashion show?"

Pennelopi managed a small nod, her voice caught in her throat. Liam, ever her spokesperson, stepped in. "Yes, this is Pennelopi Minyen. She's submitting three pieces for the Upcycled Design category."

The woman smiled warmly. "Wonderful! We've been getting some fantastic entries this year. Just need you to sign in here, and then you can take your garments to the staging area. Someone will be there to help you hang them." She gestured towards a roped-off section further into the hall.

Pennelopi signed her name, her hand trembling slightly, the pen feeling impossibly heavy. As she walked towards the staging area, she tried to keep her gaze fixed forward, but her eyes couldn't help but flick to the other displays.

There was a girl with perfectly coiffed blonde hair, meticulously pinning a dress made entirely of repurposed plastic bottles. The dress shimmered under the lights, its translucent scales catching the light, undeniably innovative. Another contestant, a boy with an edgy haircut and an air of artistic intensity, was arranging a collection of garments made from old bicycle inner tubes and reflective safety vests, creating a striking, almost cyberpunk aesthetic. Their materials, while upcycled, seemed to scream "high concept," "expensive," "cutting-edge."

Pennelopi's heart sank a little further. Her denim and lace, her canvas and handkerchiefs, felt suddenly… humble. Patchwork. Homemade. Would they be seen as less sophisticated, less "designer" than these bold, almost industrial creations? She felt a familiar wave of self-doubt wash over her, threatening to drown the fragile hope she had nurtured.

"Don't compare yourself, Pen," Liam whispered, as if reading her mind. "Their stuff is cool, sure, but yours has heart. It has a story. And it's actually *wearable*." He gave her a reassuring squeeze on the arm.

They reached the staging area, a large, well-lit space with racks and mannequins. Another volunteer, a young man with a friendly smile, directed them to an empty section. "Just hang your pieces here. The judges will be doing their initial review shortly."

Pennelopi carefully unzipped her garment bags. First, the "phoenix dress." She lifted it out, the denim layers rustling softly, the lace bodice shimmering. She hung it on a sturdy rack, stepping back to admire it. Even in the harsh fluorescent light of the staging area, it held a quiet dignity, a testament to its transformation. Then came the "Urban Bloom" jacket and skirt, their architectural forms and vibrant floral bursts making a bold statement. Finally, the "Comfort Reimagined" loungewear, its soft knits inviting touch.

As she arranged the pieces, she noticed a few other contestants glancing her way. Some looked curious, a few looked dismissive, and one girl, with a perfectly tailored upcycled blazer made from vintage suits, gave her a condescending smirk. Pennelopi felt her cheeks burn. She quickly finished arranging her garments, trying to make herself as small and unnoticeable as possible.

"Okay, they're beautiful, Pen," Liam said, pulling out his camera. "Now, let me get some shots before the crowds really come in." He began circling her display, his lens clicking, capturing the textures and details, his focused professionalism a comforting anchor in her sea of anxiety.

Just as Liam was finishing up, a hush fell over the staging area. A small group of people, clearly the judges, entered the space. They moved with an air of quiet authority, their faces serious, their clipboards clutched in their hands. Pennelopi's gaze immediately landed on one figure in particular.

Mrs. Albright.

Pennelopi knew Mrs. Albright by reputation, and occasionally by sight, from the hallways of her high school. She was the art teacher, but not the kind who encouraged free expression with glitter and finger paint. Mrs. Albright was known for her sharp tongue, her unyielding standards, and her almost brutal honesty. Her classroom was rumored to be a place of rigorous critique, where artistic weaknesses were exposed with the precision of a surgeon's scalpel. She was a woman who seemed to view art, and indeed life, with a perpetual squint of skepticism.

In person, Mrs. Albright was even more formidable than her reputation suggested. She was tall and slender, with a severe bob of iron-grey hair that framed a sharp, intelligent face. Her eyes, magnified by thick, rectangular glasses, seemed to miss nothing. She wore a tailored, dark grey suit that looked expensive despite its understated simplicity, and her posture was ramrod straight, radiating an aura of unwavering discernment. She moved through the displays with a slow, deliberate pace, her head tilted slightly, her expression unreadable. She wasn't just looking at the clothes; she seemed to be dissecting them, analyzing every stitch, every seam, every artistic choice.

Pennelopi felt a cold dread creep up her spine. Of all the judges, Mrs. Albright was the one she had hoped to avoid. Her critiques were legendary, capable of crushing even the most robust artistic egos. For someone as shy and sensitive as Pennelopi, the thought of facing her judgment was terrifying.

Mrs. Albright stopped at the plastic bottle dress, her head cocked. She ran a gloved finger over the shimmering surface, then scribbled something on her clipboard. She moved on to the bicycle inner tube collection, her lips pursed in a thoughtful line. She spent a long time at each display, sometimes leaning in close, sometimes stepping back, her gaze sweeping over the garments.

As she approached Pennelopi's section, Pennelopi felt her heart leap into her throat. She instinctively took a step back, trying to merge with the wall, to become invisible. Liam, standing beside her, subtly shifted his weight, a silent show of support.

Mrs. Albright stopped directly in front of the "phoenix dress." Her eyes, sharp and unblinking, scanned the denim layers, then moved up to the lace bodice. She didn't touch it, didn't lean in. She simply stood, observing. Pennelopi held her breath, every nerve ending screaming.

Finally, Mrs. Albright looked at her clipboard, then back at the dress. Her lips, thin and unadorned, parted. "Minyen, Pennelopi?" Her voice was low, gravelly, and carried an undeniable weight.

Pennelopi managed a tiny, almost imperceptible nod.

Mrs. Albright's gaze shifted from the dress to Pennelopi, a direct, piercing look that made Pennelopi's knees feel weak. "These are yours?" she asked, her tone devoid of emotion.

"Y-yes, ma'am," Pennelopi stammered, her voice barely a squeak.

Mrs. Albright's eyes returned to the dress. She paused for a long moment, then slowly, deliberately, she began to speak.

"The concept," she began, her voice gaining a measured cadence, "is commendable. Upcycling. Sustainable. Environmentally conscious. All very… timely." She paused, and Pennelopi felt a flicker of hope. Perhaps it wouldn't be so bad.

Then, the hammer fell.

"However," Mrs. Albright continued, her voice sharpening, "concept alone does not make art.

This... 'phoenix dress,' as you call it, is conceptually sound. But in execution?" She gestured vaguely at the garment. "It is... naïve."

The word hit Pennelopi like a physical blow. *Naïve.* It wasn't just a critique; it was a dismissal, a judgment of her skill, her understanding, her very artistic maturity.

"The denim," Mrs. Albright went on, her gaze unwavering, "while an interesting choice, lacks the fluidity required for a gown of this ambition. The layers are heavy. They fight against the desired drape. It looks... cumbersome."

Pennelopi felt a hot flush creep up her neck. She had spent *hours* trying to make the denim flow, experimenting with every cutting technique she knew. To have it dismissed as "cumbersome" felt like a direct assault on her painstaking effort.

"And the lace," Mrs. Albright continued, her voice flat. "While the individual pieces are charming, their assembly is... unrefined. The stitching is visible. The transitions are abrupt. It lacks the seamless integration one would expect from a garment aspiring to be 'wearable art.' It looks like... well, like a collection of doilies stitched together."

Pennelopi's eyes pricked with tears. *It looks like a collection of doilies stitched together.* The very thing she had tried so hard to transcend, to transform into something new, was being thrown back at her as a flaw. Her meticulous work, her careful repairs, her subtle dyeing – all dismissed.

Mrs. Albright moved on to the "Urban Bloom" jacket. "And this piece," she said, her voice tinged with a hint of something that might have been exasperation. "The canvas is stiff, almost unyielding. The flowers, while visually striking, feel… pasted on. They don't grow organically from the garment; they merely sit upon it. The juxtaposition is jarring, not harmonious. It is a bold attempt, perhaps, but ultimately, it lacks cohesion."

Pennelopi felt her shoulders slump. *Jarring. Lacks cohesion.* Every word was a fresh wound. She had poured her heart into making those flowers bloom from the rugged canvas, seeing it as a symbol of resilience and unexpected beauty. To have it called "jarring" felt like a complete misinterpretation of her artistic intent.

Finally, Mrs. Albright turned her attention to the "Comfort Reimagined" loungewear. "And this," she said, her voice softening slightly, but still critical. "The concept of comfort from repurposed knits is understandable. But the execution is... pedestrian. It looks like a collection of old sweaters sewn together. Where is the 'reimagining'? Where is the innovation? It is comfortable, yes, but it is not art. It is merely... patchwork."

Patchwork. The word, meant as a derogatory term, echoed in Pennelopi's ears. She had embraced patchwork, celebrated it, seen it as a badge of honor for upcycling. But in Mrs. Albright's mouth, it was a condemnation, a label of amateurism.

"Overall, Ms. Minyen," Mrs. Albright concluded, her gaze once again fixed on Pennelopi, "your intentions are clear. Your passion, perhaps, is evident. But your skill, your understanding of form, drape, and seamless integration, is... underdeveloped. Your designs are, at best, naïve. At worst, unrefined. You have a long way to go."

She scribbled a final note on her clipboard, then, without another word, turned and moved on to the next contestant, her other judging companions following in her wake, their expressions equally unreadable.

Pennelopi stood frozen, a statue of humiliation. The cheerful sounds of the fair, the warm light, the comforting presence of Liam – all faded into a distant, muffled roar. All she could hear were Mrs.

Albright's words, echoing in her mind: *Naïve. Unrefined. Cumbersome. Jarring. Pedestrian. Patchwork.*

She felt a wave of nausea wash over her. Her eyes, suddenly blurry, fixed on her "phoenix dress," which now, under the harsh glare of Mrs. Albright's critique, seemed to sag, its denim layers heavy, its lace bodice indeed looking like a haphazard collection of doilies. The "Urban Bloom" jacket seemed to gape, its flowers indeed pasted on. The "Comfort Reimagined" loungewear looked exactly like what it was: old sweaters sewn together.

All the weeks of painstaking work, the hours of meticulous deconstruction and reassembly, the quiet triumphs of transforming discarded materials – it all felt utterly meaningless. She had dared to dream, dared to put her heart on display, and it had been summarily, brutally, dismissed.

A hot, stinging sensation rose behind her eyes. She blinked rapidly, trying to hold back the tears that threatened to spill. She couldn't cry here, not now, not in front of everyone. The humiliation was already unbearable.

"Pen?" Liam's voice, gentle and concerned, broke through the ringing in her ears. He put a hand on her shoulder, his touch grounding. "Are you okay?"

Pennelopi shook her head, unable to speak. She felt a profound, aching emptiness. All she wanted was to disappear, to vanish into the fabric piles of her bedroom, to never show her work to anyone ever again. This was exactly what she had feared, what her shyness had always warned her against. Exposure. Judgment. And now, confirmation of her worst fears: she wasn't good enough. Her dreams were foolish. Her art was just… patchwork.

"She's just… she's tough, Pen," Liam tried to reassure her, his voice low. "Everyone knows Mrs. Albright is like that. She probably says that to everyone."

But Pennelopi knew it wasn't true. She had seen Mrs. Albright's face as she looked at the plastic bottle dress, at the bicycle inner tube collection. There had been no such harsh words, no such utter dismissal. There had been a thoughtful, discerning gaze, perhaps even a hint of respect. For Pennelopi, there had only been an unvarnished condemnation.

"I want to go home," Pennelopi whispered, her voice raw, barely audible. "I want to take them down. I want to go home."

Liam's grip on her shoulder tightened. "No, Pen. Don't. Not yet. The judging isn't over. And besides, you worked so hard. Don't let one person ruin it for you."

But it wasn't just "one person." It was Mrs. Albright, the art teacher, the arbiter of artistic merit. Her words carried weight. They resonated with Pennelopi's deepest insecurities, confirming every doubt she had ever harbored about her talent, her vision, her place in the world of art and fashion.

She stood there for what felt like an eternity, her gaze fixed on the floor, the sounds of the bustling hall a distant, mocking hum. She felt utterly defeated, stripped bare, her passion suddenly feeling like a childish delusion.

Just as she was about to insist again, to beg Liam to help her take down her pieces and leave, she felt a strange sensation. A prickle on the back of her neck. She slowly, reluctantly, lifted her head.

Mrs. Albright was standing a few feet away, her back to Pennelopi, seemingly engaged in conversation with another judge. But as Pennelopi watched, Mrs. Albright subtly shifted her weight, and her head tilted, just slightly. Her eyes, magnified by her thick glasses, flicked over her shoulder. For a fleeting, almost imperceptible moment, her gaze met Pennelopi's.

There was no warmth in those eyes, no sympathy. But there was something else. An intensity. A quiet, almost piercing observation. It wasn't the dismissive glare from moments before. It was a look that seemed to see beyond Pennelopi's slumped shoulders, beyond her tear-filled eyes, beyond the "naïve" and "unrefined" garments. It was a look that seemed to acknowledge something, to recognize a spark that even Pennelopi herself was struggling to believe in.

It was gone as quickly as it appeared. Mrs. Albright turned back to her conversation, her expression once again unreadable, her posture as rigid as ever.

Pennelopi blinked. Had she imagined it? Had the humiliation and despair made her see something that wasn't there? A desperate, fleeting hope, born from a single, intense stare.

Liam, unaware of the silent exchange, was still trying to comfort her. "Look, Pen, maybe she's just trying to push you. Maybe she sees something in you that she wants to challenge. That's what teachers do sometimes, right?"

Pennelopi didn't respond. She was still replaying that fleeting glance in her mind. It wasn't a smile. It wasn't encouragement. But it wasn't dismissal either. It was… a challenge. A silent, unspoken acknowledgment of potential, hidden beneath layers of perceived imperfection. It was a look that said, *I see you. Now, what are you going to do about it?*

The nausea subsided, replaced by a dull ache of confusion and a faint, almost imperceptible flicker of defiance. *Naïve? Unrefined?* The words still stung, but now, mixed with the sting, was a tiny spark of anger. She had poured her heart and soul into these pieces. She had seen beauty where others saw trash. She had worked tirelessly, meticulously, to transform. Was her vision truly so flawed?

She looked at her "phoenix dress" again. It still looked beautiful to her. The denim layers, heavy perhaps, but also strong, resilient. The lace, meticulously mended, telling a story of survival and renewal. It wasn't perfect in the conventional sense, but it was *hers*. It was unique. It was *her* upcycled dream.

The initial impulse to tear down her display, to retreat into the safety of her room, began to wane, replaced by a stubborn, almost defiant resolve. Mrs. Albright's words had cut deep, but that fleeting, intense stare had also planted a seed. A seed of curiosity. A seed of challenge.

What if Liam was right? What if Mrs. Albright *did* see something? What if her harshness was a test? A way to see if Pennelopi had the grit, the conviction, to stand by her artistic vision even when faced with withering criticism?

The thought was terrifying, but also exhilarating. It was a new kind of challenge, one that went beyond mastering a sewing technique or finding the perfect fabric. It was a challenge to her inner strength, to her self-belief.

She took a shaky breath, then another. The air in the mill, once thick with humiliation, now felt charged with possibility. She still wanted to disappear, but a stronger, more insistent voice within her was beginning to stir. It was the voice of the artist, the voice that had always found beauty in the discarded, the voice that refused to be silenced.

"I'm not taking them down," Pennelopi said, her voice still quiet, but firm. She looked at Liam, her eyes, though still a little watery, now held a new resolve. "I'm not giving up. Not yet."

Liam's face broke into a wide, relieved smile. "That's my Pen! I knew you wouldn't." He gave her shoulder another squeeze. "So, what now?"

Pennelopi looked back at her collection, then towards the retreating figure of Mrs. Albright, who was now deep in conversation with another judge, her back still ramrod straight. A new thought, bold and unexpected, began to form in Pennelopi's mind. If Mrs. Albright thought her work was "naïve" and "unrefined," then perhaps Mrs. Albright was exactly the person she needed to learn from. Perhaps that cynical art teacher, with her piercing gaze and brutal honesty, held the key to unlocking the next level of her artistic journey. The challenge had been issued. And Pennelopi, though still trembling, was beginning to feel a strange, exhilarating urge to accept it. The first thread of doubt had been pulled, but in its place, a stronger, more resilient thread of determination was being woven.

Chapter 4: Unlikely Alliance

The community arts center, once a beacon of hopeful creativity, now felt like a vast, echoing chamber of humiliation for Pennelopi. The cheerful chatter, the melodic strumming of the acoustic guitar, the vibrant displays of other artists – all of it seemed to mock her, amplifying the sting of Mrs. Albright's words. *Naïve. Unrefined. Cumbersome. Jarring. Pedestrian. Patchwork.* The words hammered at her, each one a fresh bruise on her already fragile artistic ego.

Liam, ever the steadfast anchor, kept a comforting hand on her shoulder. He didn't try to force conversation, sensing the raw vulnerability that radiated from her. He simply stood beside her, a silent guardian against the perceived judgment of the bustling hall. Pennelopi's eyes, still watery, darted between her own display and the retreating back of Mrs. Albright. That fleeting, intense stare from the art teacher continued to replay in her mind, a confusing counterpoint to the brutal critique. Was it a challenge, or merely a trick of the light, a figment of her desperate imagination?

The initial impulse to flee, to gather her "naïve" creations and disappear into the anonymity of her bedroom, still clawed at her. But beneath the profound shame, a tiny, stubborn ember had begun to glow. It was the ember of defiance, fueled by a quiet, simmering anger. Anger not just at Mrs. Albright's harshness, but at her own crippling shyness, at the way it allowed these words to cut so deeply, to threaten to extinguish her passion entirely.

"Pen," Liam finally said, his voice soft, "the preliminary judging is over. They're going to announce the finalists soon. Do you want to… find a quieter spot?"

Pennelopi shook her head, a slow, deliberate movement. Her gaze was fixed on Mrs. Albright, who was now standing near a display of intricate textile art, her posture as rigid and discerning as ever. A thought, audacious and terrifying, was beginning to solidify in Pennelopi's mind. If Mrs. Albright saw her as "underdeveloped," then perhaps Mrs. Albright was exactly the person she needed. The very source of her humiliation might also be the key to her growth.

"No," Pennelopi whispered, her voice still hoarse, but with a new edge of resolve. "I need to… I need to talk to her."

Liam blinked, surprised. "Mrs. Albright? Are you sure, Pen? She just… she wasn't exactly gentle."

"That's why," Pennelopi said, her voice gaining a fraction of its usual strength. "She saw something. I think. Or… she saw what I *wasn't* doing. And I need to know." The thought of approaching the formidable art teacher made her stomach clench anew, but the desire to understand, to improve, to prove her wrong – and perhaps, to prove herself right – was a stronger force than her fear.

Taking a deep, shaky breath, Pennelopi began to walk, her legs feeling like lead, towards the group of judges. Liam, sensing her determination, fell into step beside her, a silent, supportive presence. Every step felt like walking into a gale-force wind, pushing against her ingrained shyness, against the lingering echoes of Mrs. Albright's critique.

As they drew closer, Pennelopi could hear snippets of the judges' conversation. They were discussing the merits of a particularly innovative piece made from old computer circuit boards. Mrs. Albright's voice, sharp and precise, cut through the murmurs. "Technically proficient, yes. But where is the soul? The human element? It is a fascinating exercise in material manipulation, but it speaks of sterile efficiency, not art."

Pennelopi paused a few feet away, waiting for a break in the conversation. Her heart hammered against her ribs, a frantic drumbeat. She rehearsed her opening line in her head, but her mind felt like a tangled knot of yarn.

Finally, Mrs. Albright turned, her conversation with the other judge concluding. Her eyes, magnified by her glasses, swept over Pennelopi, a flicker of recognition, then a return to their usual unreadable intensity.

"Ms. Minyen," Mrs. Albright stated, her voice flat, devoid of surprise. It was as if she had expected Pennelopi to approach.

Pennelopi swallowed hard. "Mrs. Albright," she began, her voice a little shaky, "I… I heard your critique of my designs."

Mrs. Albright raised an eyebrow, a subtle gesture that nonetheless conveyed a world of skepticism. "Indeed. I was quite thorough, if I recall."

Pennelopi's cheeks flushed. "Yes, ma'am. You were. And… and it was difficult to hear. But… I also felt like… you saw something. Even if it was what was missing." She took another shaky breath, forcing herself to meet Mrs. Albright's gaze. "I want to learn. I want to understand what you meant by 'unrefined' and 'underdeveloped.' I want to be better."

The silence that followed was heavy, punctuated only by the distant hum of the fair. Mrs. Albright's expression remained impassive, her eyes unblinking. Pennelopi felt a fresh wave of despair. She was going to be dismissed again.

Then, slowly, a faint, almost imperceptible shift occurred in Mrs. Albright's eyes. A flicker of something that wasn't quite warmth, but perhaps… intrigue. "You wish to be better," Mrs. Albright repeated, her voice a low, thoughtful murmur. "Many students claim such a desire. Few possess the resilience to endure the path to true improvement."

"I… I'm willing to work," Pennelopi stammered, her voice gaining a desperate edge. "I love this. I love upcycling. I just… I don't know how to get past… the 'naïve' part."

Mrs. Albright's gaze intensified, scrutinizing Pennelopi as if she were a complex piece of art. "Your passion is evident, as I stated. But passion without discipline is merely enthusiasm. And enthusiasm, Ms. Minyen, rarely translates into mastery." She paused, then continued, her voice dropping to a conspiratorial whisper that nonetheless carried immense authority. "I saw your work. It has… potential. A raw, unpolished potential. But it is indeed raw. And unpolished. You have an eye for material, a certain ingenuity in concept. But your understanding of form, of structure, of the subtle interplay between fabric and body – it is rudimentary."

Pennelopi listened, her heart pounding, but this time, the words didn't feel like a condemnation. They felt like a diagnosis. A harsh one, but a diagnosis nonetheless. And a diagnosis implied a path to treatment, to improvement.

"I want to learn," Pennelopi reiterated, her voice firmer now. "Will you… will you teach me?"

Mrs. Albright regarded her for a long moment, a faint, almost imperceptible twitch at the corner of her lips. It wasn't a smile, not exactly, but it was a softening of her usually severe expression. "My classroom, Ms. Minyen, is not for the faint of heart. My critiques are… direct. I demand rigorous self-assessment. And I have no patience for excuses or mediocrity."

"I understand," Pennelopi said, her voice steady despite the tremor in her hands. "I'm ready to work."

Mrs. Albright's gaze flicked to Liam, who stood silently beside Pennelopi, his presence a quiet testament to his support. Then her eyes returned to Pennelopi. "Very well. Come to my classroom,

Room 307, after school on Tuesday. Bring your sketchbook. And bring that... 'phoenix dress.' We shall begin there." Her voice held a hint of a challenge, a subtle dare. "Be prepared to deconstruct everything you think you know about design, Ms. Minyen. And be prepared to work."

With that, Mrs. Albright gave a curt nod, a dismissive gesture that nonetheless felt like an acceptance. She turned and walked away, her ramrod-straight posture unwavering, leaving Pennelopi standing in the bustling hall, a strange mix of terror and exhilarating hope bubbling within her.

Liam let out a slow exhale. "Wow. She actually... she said yes. Pennelopi, that was incredible! I can't believe you did that."

Pennelopi felt a faint smile touch her lips, a genuine smile born of a quiet triumph. "I can't either," she admitted, her voice still a little breathless. The weight of humiliation had lifted, replaced by the daunting but exciting prospect of a new beginning. She had faced her fear, and it hadn't consumed her. In fact, it had opened a door.

The next few days were a nervous anticipation. Pennelopi spent hours poring over her sketchbook, looking at her designs with new, critical eyes. She saw the "naïve" elements Mrs. Albright had pointed out, the places where her ambition outstripped her technical skill. The denim dress, once a source of unadulterated pride, now seemed to reveal its flaws with painful clarity. But instead of despair, she felt a growing hunger to fix them, to truly understand the principles of design that would elevate her work from "patchwork" to "art."

Tuesday afternoon arrived, heavy with the weight of expectation. Pennelopi clutched her sketchbook and the garment bag containing the "phoenix dress" as she walked through the familiar hallways of her high school. But this time, she wasn't heading for her locker or the library. She was heading for Room 307, Mrs. Albright's art classroom, a place rumored to be both a crucible of creativity and a graveyard of artistic aspirations.

The door to Room 307 was ajar. Pennelopi pushed it open hesitantly, her heart thumping. The classroom was unlike any other she had seen. It was vast and airy, filled with the faint, earthy scent of clay and oil paint. Easels stood scattered around, some holding unfinished canvases, others empty, waiting. Sculptures, some abstract, some figurative, dotted the room. The walls were covered not with cheerful student art, but with reproductions of classical and modern masterpieces, their beauty stark and uncompromising. There was a sense of serious work here, of a profound respect for the craft.

Mrs. Albright stood by a large window, her back to the door, sketching intently in a large, leather-bound notebook. Her grey bob was neatly in place, and her posture was, as always, perfectly straight. She didn't look up as Pennelopi entered.

Pennelopi stood awkwardly by the door, unsure what to do. "Mrs. Albright?" she finally managed, her voice barely above a whisper.

Mrs. Albright slowly turned, her eyes, magnified by her glasses, fixing on Pennelopi. "Ah, Ms. Minyen. Punctual. A good start." She gestured with her pencil towards a large, empty table in the center of the room. "Place your… phoenix dress… there. And your sketchbook."

Pennelopi walked to the table, her hands trembling slightly as she carefully laid out the denim gown and her sketchbook. She stepped back, waiting.

Mrs. Albright walked over to the table, her movements precise and economical. She picked up Pennelopi's sketchbook, flipping through the pages without a word. Pennelopi held her breath, bracing herself for another round of scathing criticism.

Instead, Mrs. Albright stopped at a page, her finger tracing a delicate line. "Your lines are clean. Your concepts, as I said, show ingenuity. But your understanding of the human form, of how fabric interacts with it, is still… theoretical. You draw what you imagine, not what you *know*." She closed the sketchbook and set it down.

Then, she turned her attention to the "phoenix dress." She circled it slowly, her eyes dissecting every detail. Pennelopi felt a familiar flush of shame.

"This denim," Mrs. Albright began, her voice devoid of emotion, "it is heavy. You have attempted to make it drape like silk. It resists. This is not a flaw in the fabric, Ms. Minyen. It is a flaw in your understanding of its inherent properties." She picked up a loose denim strip. "Every material has a voice. It has a weight, a texture, a memory. You must listen to it. You must understand its limitations and its strengths. You cannot force a material to be what it is not. That is not design; that is coercion."

Pennelopi listened intently, a new concept taking root in her mind. *Listen to the material.* It was so simple, yet so profound. She had always tried to bend the fabric to her will, to force it into the shapes she envisioned. But what if the fabric itself had something to say?

"Take this dress," Mrs. Albright continued, her gaze piercing. "Unpick it. Every stitch. Deconstruct it entirely. And as you do so, pay attention. Feel the weight of each piece. Observe how it was originally cut. How it was assembled. Why it resists. Why it flows. Learn its language."

Pennelopi's eyes widened. "Unpick it? All of it?" The phoenix dress was her most ambitious piece, her pride and joy. The thought of dismantling it, of undoing weeks of painstaking work, felt like tearing a piece of herself apart.

"Yes. All of it," Mrs. Albright stated, her voice firm. "You cannot build a stronger foundation without first understanding the weaknesses of the old one. This is not destruction, Ms. Minyen. It is analysis. It is learning." She handed Pennelopi a small, sharp seam ripper. "Your first lesson begins now. Bring it back to me next Tuesday, completely deconstructed. And be prepared to tell me what you learned from its undoing."

Pennelopi left Mrs. Albright's classroom that day with a strange mix of dread and exhilaration. The task of unpicking her beloved phoenix dress felt daunting, almost sacrilegious. But Mrs. Albright's words, "Every material has a voice," resonated deeply. It was a new way of thinking about her craft, a shift from imposing her will on the fabric to collaborating with it.

The next few days were a blur of meticulous deconstruction. In her room, surrounded by the familiar scent of old cotton, Pennelopi began the painstaking process of dismantling the phoenix dress. Each stitch unpicked was an act of both undoing and discovery. She felt the weight of the denim layers, now separated, lighter, more fluid. She examined the lace doilies, no longer a cohesive bodice, but individual pieces, each with its own delicate pattern. She noticed the subtle ways the original garments had been cut, the grain lines, the hidden darts that gave them shape. She saw where her own stitching had been too tight, too visible, where her transitions had indeed been "abrupt."

It was a humbling experience, but also an incredibly insightful one. She found herself understanding, truly understanding, what Mrs. Albright had meant by "cumbersome" and "unrefined." The denim, when layered too thickly, did indeed fight against the drape. The lace, when stitched together without careful consideration of its natural flow, did lose its delicate charm. She began to see the dress not as a failure, but as a blueprint for future improvement, a lesson in material properties and construction.

When she returned to Mrs. Albright's classroom the following Tuesday, she brought not just the neatly folded piles of deconstructed denim and lace, but also a new, thicker sketchbook filled with detailed notes and small, experimental sketches of how she would approach similar challenges differently.

Mrs. Albright examined the piles of fabric, then picked up Pennelopi's new sketchbook. She flipped through the pages, her eyes scanning the detailed observations. "So, Ms. Minyen," she said, her voice still measured, "what did you learn from the undoing?"

Pennelopi took a deep breath. "I learned that denim, while strong, needs to be handled differently for drape. Maybe lighter washes, or cutting on the bias. And the lace… it needs to be integrated more seamlessly, perhaps with a sheer backing, or by carefully matching patterns so the joins disappear." She spoke with a newfound confidence, her voice clearer than it had been at the fair, her eyes meeting Mrs. Albright's gaze. She was talking about *her* work, *her* discoveries, and the words flowed more easily.

A faint, almost imperceptible nod from Mrs. Albright. "Good. You are beginning to listen. Now, for your next task." She walked over to a large, cork board covered with images. They were not fashion photos, but architectural blueprints, anatomical sketches, and photographs of natural forms – the spiral of a seashell, the branching of a tree, the intricate structure of a spiderweb.

"Design, Ms. Minyen," Mrs. Albright stated, her voice resonating with authority, "is not merely about aesthetics. It is about structure. Form. Function. The human body is a complex piece of architecture. Fabric must respond to it, flow with it, enhance it. For the next week, you will study form. You will sketch the human skeleton. You will draw the musculature. You will understand the underlying structure of the body. You will visit the botanical gardens and sketch the branching patterns of trees, the unfurling of leaves. You will go to the library and study architectural blueprints. You will understand how things are built, how they hold together, how they move. And then, you will apply that understanding to how fabric drapes, how it creates volume, how it moves with the body."

Pennelopi was taken aback. This was not what she expected. She thought they would be sewing, cutting patterns. But Mrs. Albright was asking her to delve into anatomy, botany, architecture. It was overwhelming, yet strangely exhilarating. It was a challenge that pushed her far beyond her comfort zone, forcing her to see design not just as a creative impulse, but as a rigorous, intellectual discipline.

The following weeks were a whirlwind of unconventional lessons. Mrs. Albright pushed Pennelopi relentlessly, but always with a purpose. She taught Pennelopi to see the world through a designer's eyes, to find inspiration in unexpected places. They visited art galleries, not to admire the paintings, but to analyze the drapery in classical sculptures, the way light played on folds of fabric in Renaissance portraits. Mrs. Albright would quiz Pennelopi, demanding detailed observations. "How does the sculptor convey the weight of the fabric? What is the underlying structure of that gown? How does the artist use light and shadow to create volume?"

They spent hours in the botanical gardens, Pennelopi sketching furiously as Mrs. Albright pointed out the intricate patterns of growth, the way a leaf unfurled, the elegant curve of a branch. "Nature is the ultimate designer, Ms. Minyen," Mrs. Albright would say. "Observe its efficiency, its beauty, its inherent logic. Apply that logic to your seams, to your cuts, to your construction."

Mrs. Albright also introduced Pennelopi to the history of fashion, not through glossy magazines, but through dense, academic texts. She made Pennelopi analyze historical garments, dissecting their construction, understanding how societal norms and technological advancements shaped their forms. "You cannot innovate, Ms. Minyen," Mrs. Albright would state, "if you do not understand the foundations upon which innovation is built."

Pennelopi found herself spending more time in the library, poring over books on anatomy and architecture, sketching skeletons and building plans, trying to understand the fundamental principles of structure and form. Her sketchbook, once filled with fantastical, imaginative designs, now contained meticulous studies of bones, muscles, and the blueprints of ancient cathedrals. It was a grueling, intellectually demanding process, far more rigorous than she had anticipated. There were moments of frustration, when her mind felt overwhelmed, when she questioned if she was truly capable of grasping these complex concepts.

But Mrs. Albright, despite her cynical demeanor, was a surprisingly patient and insightful teacher. She never offered praise easily, but a rare, almost imperceptible nod, a flicker of approval in her eyes, was more rewarding than any effusive compliment. She pushed Pennelopi, but she also provided the tools and the intellectual framework for growth. She didn't just tell Pennelopi what was wrong; she showed her *why* it was wrong, and *how* to make it right.

Slowly, imperceptibly at first, Pennelopi began to change. Her shyness, while still present, began to recede in the face of her burgeoning knowledge and confidence. She found herself speaking up more in Mrs. Albright's classroom, asking questions, offering observations, her voice clearer, more assured. She was no longer just a quiet girl who sewed; she was a student, an apprentice, a designer in training.

One afternoon, Mrs. Albright gave Pennelopi a new assignment. "You have studied form. You have observed nature. Now, you will create. You will take these scraps," she gestured to a pile of seemingly random fabric remnants – a piece of old burlap, a strip of worn velvet, a section of torn silk lining – "and you will create a garment that embodies the concept of 'tension and release.' You will use the inherent properties of these disparate materials to tell a story of opposing forces, and how they can be brought into harmony."

Pennelopi stared at the pile, a daunting challenge. Burlap and velvet? Roughness and luxury? But then, she remembered Mrs. Albright's words: "Every material has a voice." She began to experiment, draping the burlap, feeling its stiffness, its resistance. She then draped the velvet, luxuriating in its softness, its fluidity. She saw the potential for contrast, for a dialogue between the two.

She spent the next week immersed in the project, her room once again a whirlwind of creative energy. She cut the burlap into sharp, geometric panels, creating a rigid, almost architectural base. Then, she used the velvet to create soft, flowing elements that seemed to spill from the burlap, a cascade of luxurious folds that contrasted sharply with the rough texture. The torn silk lining, instead of being hidden, became a delicate, almost ethereal layer, peeking out from beneath the heavier fabrics, symbolizing vulnerability and hidden beauty.

When she presented the finished garment to Mrs. Albright, it was a striking, almost sculptural piece – a tunic that was both rigid and flowing, harsh and soft, a testament to the power of contrast and the unexpected harmony that could be found in opposing forces.

Mrs. Albright walked around the tunic, her eyes scrutinizing every detail. Pennelopi held her breath, bracing herself for the inevitable critique.

Mrs. Albright finally stopped, her gaze fixed on a particularly intricate seam where the burlap met the velvet. She reached out, her gloved finger tracing the line. "The stitching," she said, her voice a low murmur, "is precise. The transitions, while still evident, are no longer abrupt. You have begun to understand the language of materials, Ms. Minyen. You have begun to listen."

Pennelopi felt a warmth spread through her, a quiet triumph. It wasn't praise, not exactly, but it was an acknowledgment of growth, of progress. Mrs. Albright's eyes, usually so critical, held a flicker of something akin to satisfaction.

"This piece," Mrs. Albright continued, "is not merely 'patchwork.' It is a conversation. A dialogue between textures, between forms, between ideas. You are beginning to find your voice, Ms. Minyen. A voice that is unique. A voice that speaks of ingenuity and passion. But also, now, a voice that speaks of understanding. Of discipline."

Pennelopi felt a surge of emotion. Mrs. Albright, the cynical art teacher, had just called her work a "conversation." She had acknowledged her "voice." It was more than she could have ever hoped for.

The mentorship continued, a challenging but profoundly rewarding journey. Mrs. Albright pushed

Pennelopi to think beyond the needle and thread, to understand the broader context of art and design. She made Pennelopi research social movements and their impact on fashion, analyze the psychology of color, and even explore the mathematical principles behind pattern making. It was a holistic education, designed not just to teach her how to sew, but how to *think* like a designer.

And slowly, almost imperceptibly, the cynical art teacher began to reveal glimpses of the passionate artist beneath the stern exterior. Mrs. Albright would sometimes share anecdotes from her own past, subtle hints of a time when she, too, was a struggling artist, facing skepticism and challenges. She never offered explicit sympathy, but her shared experiences, her quiet understanding of the artistic struggle, forged a bond between them. Pennelopi began to see Mrs. Albright not just as a formidable mentor, but as a complex, deeply dedicated artist who, in her own way, was trying to nurture the same fire she possessed.

Pennelopi's personal growth mirrored her artistic development. As her understanding of design deepened, so did her confidence. She found herself less afraid to express her opinions, to defend her artistic choices. Her shyness, once a suffocating cloak, became more like a comfortable shawl – still present, but no longer debilitating. She learned to stand up for her artistic vision, not with loud pronouncements, but with the quiet conviction that came from deep understanding and meticulous craftsmanship.

She began to understand that true style wasn't about money or expensive materials. It was about ingenuity, about passion, about seeing the potential in the overlooked, and about the discipline to transform that potential into something meaningful. Mrs. Albright had taught her that. She had taken a "naïve" and "unrefined" girl and, through relentless challenge and uncompromising honesty, had begun to forge her into a true designer. The journey was far from over, but Pennelopi knew, with a quiet certainty, that she was finally on the right path. The unlikely alliance had been forged, and the threads of her upcycled dream were growing stronger, more intricate, more resilient with every stitch.

Chapter 5: The Cutting Edge

The air in Mrs. Albright's art classroom, Room 307, had always held the faint, earthy scent of clay and oil paint. But for Pennelopi, it now carried a new, exhilarating aroma – the scent of challenge, of discovery, of disciplined creation. The "tension and release" tunic, a striking piece born from burlap, velvet, and silk lining, stood on a mannequin in the corner, a silent testament to her burgeoning understanding. Mrs. Albright's rare, almost imperceptible nod of approval had been more potent than any effusive praise, a quiet affirmation that Pennelopi was, indeed, beginning to listen to the language of materials.

The mentorship that followed was relentless, uncompromising, and utterly transformative. Mrs. Albright was not merely a teacher; she was a sculptor of minds, chipping away at Pennelopi's preconceived notions, her self-doubt, and her technical limitations with the precision of a master artisan. There were no easy answers, no shortcuts, only rigorous inquiry and demanding practice.

One afternoon, Mrs. Albright laid out a series of photographs on the large central table. They depicted not fashion, but ancient Greek and Roman sculptures, their marble drapery flowing with impossible grace. "Observe, Ms. Minyen," Mrs. Albright commanded, her voice low and resonant. "The ancients understood fabric. They understood how gravity acts upon it, how it gathers, how it falls. They understood the interplay of light and shadow on its folds, how it can reveal and conceal the form beneath. Your challenge this week: to create a garment, using only white muslin, that captures the essence of this classical drapery. No seams where a seam is not absolutely necessary. No embellishments. Only form. Only flow. Only light."

Pennelopi stared at the images, her mind reeling. Muslin, a simple, unadorned fabric, was to become a medium for sculptural expression. It was a daunting task, stripping away all her usual tricks of patchwork and juxtaposition, forcing her to confront the fundamental principles of drape and form. She spent hours in her room, the white muslin a blank canvas. She draped it, twisted it, gathered it, pinned it, unpinned it. She studied her own reflection in the mirror, observing how her clothes moved with her body, how light caught the fabric. She experimented with bias cuts, understanding how the diagonal grain of the fabric allowed for greater fluidity. She learned to manipulate the fabric with her hands, coaxing it into graceful cascades, understanding its weight, its inherent resistance, its potential for ethereal beauty.

When she presented her muslin creation to Mrs. Albright, it was a revelation. It wasn't a finished garment in the traditional sense, but a masterfully draped piece that flowed around the mannequin like liquid, its folds catching the light in a myriad of subtle ways. Mrs. Albright circled it slowly, her eyes, usually so critical, holding a flicker of genuine appreciation. "You are beginning to understand the dance between fabric and form, Ms. Minyen," she said, her voice a rare murmur of approval. "The muslin speaks. And you, finally, are listening."

This lesson, and many others like it, pushed Pennelopi to think beyond the literal act of sewing. Mrs. Albright forced her to dissect the *why* behind every design choice. They delved into the psychology of color, analyzing how different hues evoked specific emotions and perceptions. Pennelopi learned that the faded blues of her denim, once a limitation, could evoke a sense of history, of comfort, of resilience. The vibrant bursts of color from her silk scraps, when strategically placed, could draw the eye, create a focal point, or infuse a sense of playful energy.

They explored the history of fashion, not as a parade of changing styles, but as a reflection of societal shifts, technological advancements, and cultural narratives. Mrs. Albright would assign dense readings on everything from the elaborate corsetry of the Victorian era to the minimalist designs of the 20th century. "You cannot truly innovate, Ms. Minyen," she would often state, "if you do not understand the foundations upon which innovation is built. Every stitch, every silhouette, every embellishment carries a historical weight, a cultural resonance. To ignore it is to design in a vacuum." Pennelopi found herself spending more and more time in the library, poring over academic texts, filling notebooks with timelines and analyses, her mind expanding with each new discovery.

The mathematical principles behind pattern making, once a daunting mystery, slowly began to reveal their inherent logic. Mrs. Albright introduced her to the intricacies of drafting patterns, teaching her how to translate a three-dimensional concept into a two-dimensional blueprint. Pennelopi learned about darts, pleats, and gathers, not just as techniques, but as tools to shape fabric, to create volume, to flatter the human form. She spent hours meticulously drawing patterns on brown paper, her ruler and French curves becoming extensions of her hand. The precision required was immense, a stark contrast to the free-form draping she had initially favored,

but it instilled in her a profound respect for the underlying structure of garment construction.

Her room, once a chaotic but familiar sanctuary, transformed into a veritable design studio. The piles of fabric became more organized, sorted not just by color, but by weight, drape, and fiber content. Her desk, usually buried under a cheerful mess, now held neatly stacked pattern blocks, rolls of tracing paper, and a growing collection of specialized tools. The vintage Singer sewing machine, once a simple workhorse, became a precision instrument under her increasingly skilled hands. She learned to adjust its tension with expert finesse, to choose the right needle for every fabric, to execute stitches that were so fine, they almost disappeared into the material.

The process of deconstruction, once a means to an end, became an art form in itself. Pennelopi no longer just unpicked seams; she dissected garments, analyzing their construction with the eye of an engineer. She learned to identify the subtle differences in a sleeve set, the variations in a collar stand, the clever ways designers had manipulated fabric to achieve specific effects. This deep understanding of garment anatomy informed her own designs, allowing her to build her upcycled pieces with a newfound structural integrity. She began to see the "bones" of clothing, the underlying architecture that gave them shape and longevity.

Her designs, once dismissed as "patchwork," began to evolve. They still celebrated the beauty of discarded materials, but they did so with a sophistication and intentionality that had previously been lacking. Her "Upcycled Dream" collection, initially conceived for the local show, now became a living, breathing entity, constantly being refined and reimagined.

She revisited the "phoenix dress," the very piece Mrs. Albright had so brutally critiqued. Armed with her new knowledge of drape and material properties, she began to reconstruct it. She chose lighter-weight denims for the cascading layers, cutting them on the bias to enhance their fluidity. The lace bodice, instead of being simply stitched together, was now meticulously appliquéd onto a sheer, recycled silk lining, creating a seamless, almost ethereal effect. The mismatched buttons, once merely decorative, were now strategically placed to create subtle visual rhythms, drawing the eye along the lines of the garment. The result was a gown that retained its original concept of transformation but now possessed an undeniable elegance, a quiet power that spoke of mastery.

The "Urban Bloom" jacket also underwent a radical transformation. Instead of simply "pasting on" the fabric flowers, Pennelopi learned to integrate them organically into the canvas. She experimented with three-dimensional fabric manipulation techniques, creating flowers that seemed to emerge from the jacket itself, their petals folding and unfolding with a lifelike quality. The juxtaposition of rugged canvas and delicate blooms was no longer "jarring," but a deliberate, harmonious dialogue between opposing forces, embodying the concept of nature reclaiming the urban landscape with a newfound artistic maturity. She even incorporated subtle architectural lines into the jacket's silhouette, a direct application of her studies in form and structure.

And the "Comfort Reimagined" loungewear, once "pedestrian," became a study in understated luxury. Pennelopi learned to blend the various knits with such seamless precision that the patchwork effect was elevated to a sophisticated textural play. She focused on the inherent softness and drape of the materials, creating silhouettes that were both comfortable and elegant. Subtle, hand-stitched details, inspired by her study of historical embroidery, elevated the pieces, transforming them from simple loungewear into truly reimagined garments that spoke of quiet indulgence and sustainable chic.

As her artistic skills deepened, so did Pennelopi's personal confidence. The shyness, once a suffocating cloak, began to feel more like a comfortable shawl – still present, but no longer debilitating. In Mrs. Albright's classroom, she found her voice, not through forced extroversion, but through the quiet authority of knowledge and skill. She began to ask questions, to offer observations, to articulate her design choices with a clarity and conviction that surprised even herself. She learned to defend her artistic vision, not with emotional pleas, but with reasoned arguments grounded in principles of design, material science, and historical context.

The fear of judgment, while not entirely gone, began to recede. She still felt nervous when presenting her work, but the knowledge that she had poured every ounce of her intellect and skill into each piece, that she had listened to the materials, understood the forms, and applied rigorous discipline, gave her a new kind of courage. She was no longer just a girl who sewed; she was a designer, an artist, and she had something important to say through her creations.

Liam, her ever-present confidant, observed this transformation with a quiet awe. He still came over almost daily, but now, instead of just offering encouragement, he became a collaborator. He would discuss design concepts with her, offering insights from his photographer's eye. He'd capture the evolving beauty of her pieces with his camera, his lens documenting her journey from "naïve" to "masterful."

"You know, Pen," he said one afternoon, watching her meticulously hand-stitch a delicate detail onto the reconstructed phoenix dress, "you're different. You're… sharper. More confident. It's like Mrs. Albright didn't just teach you how to sew; she taught you how to *see*."

Pennelopi looked up, a faint smile touching her lips. "She taught me how to listen," she corrected, her gaze drifting to the pile of fabric scraps, no longer just discarded remnants, but a symphony of potential. "To the fabric. To the form. To the history. And… to myself."

Mrs. Albright, for her part, maintained her cynical exterior, but subtle shifts in her demeanor hinted at a deeper connection. She would sometimes share anecdotes from her own past, subtle glimpses into her own artistic journey, revealing a vulnerability that Pennelopi had never expected. She spoke of her own struggles with artistic vision, of the relentless pursuit of mastery, of the sacrifices required to truly dedicate oneself to a craft. These shared moments, unspoken understandings of the artistic struggle, forged a profound bond between them, a mentor-mentee relationship built on mutual respect and a shared passion for the uncompromising pursuit of art.

One evening, as Pennelopi was packing up her tools after a particularly intense session in Mrs. Albright's classroom, the teacher paused by the door, her hand on the light switch. "Ms. Minyen," she said, her voice softer than usual, "true style is not about fleeting trends or superficial adornment. It is about ingenuity. It is about passion. And it is about the discipline to transform raw material, whether it be canvas or concept, into something that speaks of truth and beauty." She paused, her eyes, magnified by her glasses, meeting Pennelopi's. "You are beginning to understand that, Ms. Minyen. You are beginning to find your edge."

The words resonated deeply within Pennelopi. *The cutting edge.* It wasn't just about sharp scissors or precise seams. It was about the edge of innovation, the edge of understanding, the edge of her own evolving self. She had entered Mrs. Albright's classroom a shy, "naïve" girl, her dreams fragile, her skills underdeveloped. She was emerging, slowly but surely, as a designer in her own right, armed with knowledge, discipline, and a quiet, unwavering confidence. The journey was far from over, but Pennelopi knew, with a quiet certainty, that she was finally on the right path. The threads of her upcycled dream were no longer just being woven; they were being honed, sharpened, transformed into something truly extraordinary.

Chapter 6: Runway Jitters

The weeks following Pennelopi's intense mentorship with Mrs. Albright blurred into a singular, focused pursuit of artistic mastery. Her room, once a sanctuary of private creation, now hummed with a different kind of energy – the purposeful hum of a professional studio, albeit a small, upcycled one. The "tension and release" tunic, the refined "phoenix dress," the re-sculpted "Urban Bloom" jacket, and the elevated "Comfort Reimagined" loungewear all stood on mannequins, silent witnesses to her transformation. Each stitch, each seam, each carefully chosen scrap of fabric whispered of Mrs. Albright's lessons: the language of materials, the principles of form and function, the discipline required to translate passion into mastery.

Pennelopi's hands, once prone to trembling with nerves, now moved with a quiet, assured precision. She could deconstruct a garment with the speed and accuracy of a surgeon, understanding its every bone and muscle. Her patterns, once rudimentary, were now meticulously drafted, anticipating the fabric's drape and the body's movement. She had learned to listen, truly listen, to the materials, coaxing their inherent properties into harmonious forms rather than forcing them into preconceived notions. The "patchwork" of her early days had evolved into a sophisticated tapestry of textures and narratives, each piece telling a story of resilience and reimagination.

Her personal growth mirrored her artistic development. The crippling shyness, while not entirely vanquished, had receded significantly. In Mrs. Albright's classroom, she had found her voice, not through forced extroversion, but through the quiet authority of knowledge and skill. She could articulate her design choices with clarity, defend her artistic vision with reasoned arguments, and engage in intellectual discussions about art and fashion without her voice faltering or her cheeks burning. She still preferred quiet observation to boisterous chatter, but the fear of being seen, of being judged, had lessened, replaced by a burgeoning confidence in her own capabilities.

But as the date of the "Green Stitch" Upcycled Fashion Show loomed closer, a familiar, insidious dread began to creep back in. It started subtly, a faint flutter in her stomach when she saw a poster for the event, a tightening in her chest when Liam mentioned the number of tickets sold. The analytical, disciplined part of her brain, honed by Mrs. Albright, understood the principles of design.

But the emotional, vulnerable part of her, the part that had always hidden behind thick glasses and quiet murmurs, began to feel the immense pressure of public exposure once more.

This wasn't Mrs. Albright's classroom, where critique was a tool for growth, delivered by a mentor who saw her potential. This was a public stage. A competition. A place where her art would be judged not just by discerning eyes, but by a general audience, by her peers, by people who might not understand the philosophy behind upcycling, who might only see "old clothes."

The thought of standing on that stage, of having to speak about her collection, made her throat constrict. All the practice sessions with Liam, all the newfound confidence she had gained in Mrs. Albright's presence, seemed to evaporate under the looming shadow of the runway. She was still Pennelopi, the girl who struggled to make eye contact, the girl who felt most at home in the quiet solitude of her room, surrounded by her fabrics.

Liam, ever perceptive, noticed her growing anxiety. He would find her sometimes, late at night, hunched over her sewing machine, not working, but simply staring at a piece of fabric, her brow furrowed in thought. "Still got those jitters, Pen?" he'd ask gently, sitting on the edge of her bed.

"More than jitters, Liam," she confessed one evening, her voice barely a whisper. "It's… it's like my brain knows I can do this, but my body just wants to run and hide. What if I freeze? What if I can't speak? What if they laugh?"

Liam would offer his usual steady reassurance. "No one's going to laugh, Pen. Your designs are incredible. And you've practiced your presentation a hundred times. You'll be great. Just focus on the clothes. Let them speak for you." He'd pull out his camera, showing her the stunning, professional-quality photos he had taken of her finished pieces. "Look at these, Pen. This is what they're going to see. Not just old fabric, but art. Your art."

But the external validation, while comforting, couldn't entirely quell the internal turmoil. Pennelopi found herself obsessing over every detail, re-checking seams, re-pressing fabrics, convinced that any tiny imperfection would be magnified under the stage lights, confirming Mrs. Albright's initial assessment of "unrefined." She wanted her collection to be perfect, not just for the judges, but for herself, a tangible proof that she had overcome her limitations.

The day of the "Green Stitch" Upcycled Fashion Show dawned bright and clear, a cruel contrast to the storm brewing in Pennelopi's stomach. The community arts center, the old textile mill, was abuzz with a nervous energy that mirrored her own. Finalists were arriving, models were being prepped, and the main hall was slowly filling with spectators.

Pennelopi arrived with Liam, her parents, and even a very excited Leo, who was convinced his sister was about to become a "fashion superhero." Her three models, friends from school Liam had recruited, met them at the staging area. They were enthusiastic and supportive, but their presence, and the need to direct them, only added to Pennelopi's mounting anxiety.

The staging area was a chaotic symphony of buzzing hair dryers, snapping camera flashes, and the low murmur of conversations. Models practiced their walks, designers made last-minute adjustments, and volunteers rushed around with clipboards. The air was thick with the scent of hairspray, makeup, and nervous anticipation.

Pennelopi's eyes darted around, taking in the other contestants. Many of the same faces from the preliminary judging were there, their displays now fully realized. The girl with the plastic bottle dress had added intricate LED lights, making her creation shimmer with an almost otherworldly glow. The boy with the bicycle inner tube collection had incorporated sound elements, his models walking to a rhythmic, industrial beat. Their creations were undeniably impressive, bold, and seemed to scream "professional."

Pennelopi looked at her own collection: the flowing denim of the phoenix dress, the architectural canvas of the Urban Bloom jacket, the soft luxury of the Comfort Reimagined loungewear. They were beautiful, she knew. They were a testament to her growth, to Mrs. Albright's lessons. But next to the dazzling, high-concept displays of her competitors, they felt… quiet. Humble. She worried they would be overlooked, dismissed as too simple, too "upcycled" in a way that implied less, not more.

"You look amazing, Pen," her model, Maya, said, her voice cheerful as Pennelopi made a final adjustment to the neckline of the phoenix dress. "This dress is stunning. I feel like a queen."

Pennelopi managed a weak smile. "Thanks, Maya. Just… try to make the denim flow, okay? It's heavier than it looks."

As the minutes ticked by, Pennelopi felt the familiar tightening in her chest, the prickle of heat on her skin. Her shyness, which she had worked so hard to overcome, threatened to engulf her entirely. She felt a desperate urge to bolt, to hide, to simply disappear.

Then, a familiar, measured voice cut through the backstage chaos. "Ms. Minyen."

Pennelopi turned, her heart leaping into her throat. Mrs. Albright stood a few feet away, her arms crossed, her gaze sweeping over Pennelopi's collection. She wore a dark, impeccably tailored suit, and her grey bob was, as always, perfectly in place. Her expression was unreadable, but her presence alone commanded attention.

"Your models are prepared?" Mrs. Albright asked, her voice flat.

Pennelopi nodded, her throat suddenly dry. "Yes, ma'am."

Mrs. Albright walked closer, her eyes scrutinizing the phoenix dress. She didn't touch it, but her gaze was intense, dissecting every detail. Pennelopi braced herself for a final, pre-show critique, a reminder of her lingering imperfections.

Instead, Mrs. Albright's eyes flicked to Pennelopi, a direct, piercing look. "You have worked diligently, Ms. Minyen. You have listened. You have learned. You have transformed." Her voice was low, almost a murmur, but it carried an undeniable weight. "Your designs are no longer merely 'patchwork.' They are a conversation. A dialogue between textures, between forms, between ideas. They speak of ingenuity. Of passion. And now, of understanding. Of discipline."

Pennelopi stared at her, stunned. It was the same assessment she had given her after the "tension and release" tunic, but hearing it now, in the chaotic, high-pressure environment of the fashion show, it felt like a profound validation. It wasn't effusive praise, but it was Mrs. Albright's highest form of acknowledgment.

"Remember, Ms. Minyen," Mrs. Albright continued, her voice gaining a subtle edge, "true style is not about money. It is about vision. About integrity. Your work possesses both. Let it speak for itself. And when it is your turn to speak, remember the story you are telling. The story of transformation. The story of the overlooked. The story of your own upcycled dream." She paused, then added, almost as an afterthought, "And do not slouch. Stand tall. Your work deserves it."

With that, Mrs. Albright gave a curt nod, a dismissive gesture that nonetheless felt like a powerful endorsement. She turned and walked away, her ramrod-straight posture unwavering, disappearing into the bustling crowd.

Pennelopi stood rooted to the spot, a strange mix of awe and renewed determination flooding through her. Mrs. Albright's words, delivered with her characteristic bluntness, had cut through the fog of her anxiety, anchoring her. She had seen the transformation, not just in the fabric, but in Pennelopi herself.

"Okay, Pennelopi, five minutes!" a volunteer called out, her voice urgent. "Models to the entrance!"

Pennelopi took a deep, shaky breath. Her heart was still pounding, but the frantic rhythm had settled into a more steady beat. She looked at her models, then at her collection, then at Liam, who gave her a reassuring thumbs-up.

"You got this, Pen," Liam mouthed, his eyes full of belief.

The lights in the main hall dimmed, and a hush fell over the audience. The music changed, shifting from cheerful folk to a more dramatic, anticipatory beat. Pennelopi felt a surge of adrenaline. This was it.

She watched as the first model, not one of hers, stepped onto the runway, bathed in a spotlight. The plastic bottle dress shimmered, its LED lights twinkling. The audience gasped, then applauded.

Then came the announcement. "Next up, representing the 'Upcycled Design' category, we have Pennelopi Minyen, with her collection, 'The Upcycled Dream'!"

Pennelopi's breath hitched. Her stomach lurched. Her model, Maya, in the phoenix dress, took a deep breath, and with a graceful step, walked onto the runway.

The spotlight hit her. The denim layers of the phoenix dress, now expertly cut and draped, rippled and flowed with an unexpected elegance. The lace bodice, meticulously appliquéd, shimmered delicately. The audience, initially murmuring, fell silent. Then, a ripple of quiet appreciation spread through the hall. A few murmurs of "Wow," "Look at that," "That's denim?" could be heard.

Pennelopi watched, her heart in her throat. Maya walked with confidence, the dress moving with her, a testament to Pennelopi's newfound understanding of drape and form. It wasn't just "patchwork." It was art. It was her upcycled dream, finally taking flight.

A strange, exhilarating warmth spread through Pennelopi. The fear was still there, a tiny tremor, but it was overshadowed by a profound sense of pride. Her designs, her vision, her transformation – they were finally being seen. And they were speaking for themselves, eloquently, beautifully, on the runway. The cutting edge, indeed.

The phoenix dress completed its circuit, Maya exiting to a wave of applause that felt, to Pennelopi, like the sweetest music. Next came the "Urban Bloom" jacket and skirt. Her model, Chloe, strode onto the runway with an air of confident defiance. The architectural lines of the canvas jacket, softened by the organically integrated fabric flowers, created a striking silhouette. The vibrant bursts of color from the silk and embroidered patches seemed to pulse under the lights. This piece, a dialogue between ruggedness and delicate beauty, drew gasps from the audience. Pennelopi saw heads nodding, heard whispers of "ingenious" and "so creative." The juxtaposition, once "jarring" in Mrs. Albright's initial critique, was now clearly understood as a deliberate artistic choice, a testament to Pennelopi's refined vision.

Finally, it was Liam's turn to shine, not as a model, but as the photographer capturing the moment. He had positioned himself strategically at the end of the runway, his camera clicking furiously, capturing every angle, every detail, every subtle shift in light on Pennelopi's creations. He was documenting her triumph, his lens a silent witness to her journey.

The last of Pennelopi's pieces, the "Comfort Reimagined" loungewear, floated onto the runway on her third model, Sarah. The soft, blended knits, once dismissed as "pedestrian," now exuded an understated luxury. The seamless precision of the patchwork, the subtle textural play, and the elegant drape of the fabric spoke of quiet indulgence and sophisticated design. The audience, accustomed to flashy, elaborate runway pieces, seemed captivated by its quiet elegance, its unexpected chicness. It was a powerful statement about finding beauty and luxury in simplicity, in sustainability.

As Sarah exited the runway, the applause for Pennelopi's collection swelled, a genuine, sustained ovation that filled the vast hall. It wasn't just polite applause; it was an acknowledgment of something truly unique, something that resonated with the spirit of the "Green Stitch" show. Pennelopi felt a wave of relief, so profound it almost brought her to her knees. She had done it. Her designs had spoken.

Now came the moment she had dreaded the most: the designer's presentation.

"And now," the announcer's voice boomed, "please welcome to the stage, the designer of 'The Upcycled Dream' collection, Pennelopi Minyen!"

Pennelopi's heart leaped into her throat. Her legs felt like jelly. Every fiber of her being screamed at her to run, to hide. She could feel all eyes on her, the collective gaze of the audience a heavy weight. The stage lights, which had illuminated her designs so beautifully, now felt like blinding interrogators.

Liam, standing beside her, gave her a gentle nudge. "Go on, Pen. You got this. Remember what Mrs. Albright said. Stand tall."

Pennelopi took a shaky breath, then another. She straightened her shoulders, remembering Mrs. Albright's words: *And do not slouch. Stand tall. Your work deserves it.* She imagined the confidence of the models, the poise of Mrs. Albright. She focused on the feeling of the fabric in her hands, the familiar comfort of her own creations. This wasn't about her; it was about the story she had to tell.

She walked onto the stage, her steps feeling surprisingly steady despite the tremor in her hands. The spotlight hit her, momentarily disorienting her. She could see the blurred faces of the audience, the rows of seats stretching back into the shadows. She found her parents' faces in the front row, their smiles wide and proud. She saw Liam, camera poised, his eyes full of encouragement. And in the second row, almost hidden, she saw Mrs. Albright, her expression unreadable, but her gaze fixed on Pennelopi.

Pennelopi took another deep breath, the air filling her lungs. She looked at her collection, displayed on mannequins at the back of the stage. The phoenix dress, the Urban Bloom jacket, the Comfort Reimagined loungewear. They were her anchors, her silent, eloquent companions.

"Good afternoon, everyone," Pennelopi began, her voice, to her own surprise, clear and steady, though a little soft. It wasn't the booming voice of an orator, but it was strong enough to carry across the quiet hall. "My name is Pennelopi Minyen, and this is 'The Upcycled Dream' collection."

She paused, allowing the title to resonate. She felt a wave of calm wash over her. She wasn't speaking to a faceless crowd; she was sharing her passion, her philosophy.

"This collection," she continued, her voice gaining a quiet confidence, "is a celebration of transformation. It's about finding beauty in what's often overlooked, discarded, or forgotten. It's about giving new life to old materials, proving that true style isn't about expensive fabrics or fleeting trends, but about ingenuity, creativity, and a deep respect for the resources we have."

She gestured to the phoenix dress. "This gown, for example, is made from over ten pairs of discarded denim jeans and vintage lace doilies. Each piece of denim carries its own history, its own wear. By deconstructing and meticulously reconstructing them, I wanted to create a garment that speaks of resilience, of renewal, of how something ordinary can be transformed into something extraordinary." She explained the bias cuts, the careful appliqué of the lace, the subtle placement of the mismatched buttons. As she spoke about the technical details, the intricate process, her confidence grew. This was her domain. This was what she knew.

Next, she moved to the Urban Bloom jacket. "This piece, 'Urban Bloom,' is crafted from repurposed canvas – old tarps and army surplus bags. The stiffness of the canvas allowed for architectural forms, symbolizing the urban landscape. But from this ruggedness, I wanted to show life, beauty, and growth. The fabric flowers, made from silk scarves and embroidered remnants, are integrated to appear as if they are organically emerging from the canvas, a metaphor for nature reclaiming its space, for finding softness and vibrancy in unexpected places." She described the three-dimensional fabric manipulation, the careful hand-stitching that brought the flowers to life.

Finally, she presented the Comfort Reimagined loungewear. "And this collection, 'Comfort Reimagined,' is a study in understated luxury. It's made from a variety of discarded knits – cashmere sweaters, merino wool scarves, silk pajama bottoms. The goal was to take these comfortable, familiar materials and elevate them through seamless blending and careful tailoring, creating pieces that are both incredibly comfortable and undeniably chic. It's about redefining luxury, finding it in sustainability and thoughtful design." She highlighted the subtle textural play, the hidden details.

As she spoke, Pennelopi felt the familiar tightening in her chest begin to loosen. Her voice, while still soft, was clear, passionate, and articulate. She wasn't just reciting facts; she was telling a story, her story, through her designs. She looked at the audience, and for the first time, she saw not a faceless crowd, but individuals, their faces rapt, their eyes reflecting genuine interest and admiration. She saw nods of understanding, smiles of appreciation.

When she finished, a wave of applause erupted, even louder and more enthusiastic than for the runway walk. It was a thunderous ovation, a recognition not just of her designs, but of her courage, her vision, her powerful message.

Pennelopi felt a profound sense of accomplishment, a warmth spreading through her entire being. She had faced her deepest fear, and she had not only survived, she had thrived. She had found her voice, not by forcing herself to be someone she wasn't, but by speaking her truth, by letting her passion shine through.

She looked at Mrs. Albright again. The art teacher's face was still impassive, but in her eyes, Pennelopi saw it – a flicker of pride, a subtle acknowledgment of a challenge met, a lesson learned. It was a silent conversation, a profound connection between mentor and student.

As she walked off the stage, the applause still ringing in her ears, Liam rushed forward, enveloping her in a triumphant hug. "You did it, Pen! You were amazing! You were incredible! Your voice was so clear!"

Her parents joined them, her mother's eyes brimming with tears, her father's face beaming with pride. Leo, bouncing with excitement, declared, "You're the best fashion superhero ever, Pennelopi!"

Pennelopi laughed, a genuine, unburdened sound. The weight of shyness, though still a part of her, no longer felt like a crushing burden. It was a part of her story, a part of her journey, but it no longer defined her. She had proven that true style wasn't about money, or privilege, or even innate charisma. It was about ingenuity, about passion, and about the courage to stand up for her artistic vision, to let her upcycled dream take flight. The runway jitters had been conquered, and in their place, a quiet, unwavering confidence had taken root. This was just the beginning.

Chapter 7: A Vision Unveiled

The thunderous applause that erupted as Pennelopi stepped off the stage was a physical force, a wave of sound that washed over her, obliterating the lingering echoes of her fear. It wasn't just polite clapping; it was a sustained, genuine ovation, a roar of approval that vibrated through the very floorboards of the old textile mill. Relief, so profound it almost buckled her knees, flooded her system, mingling with a heady rush of triumph. She had done it. She had faced her deepest fear, and she had not only survived, but she had soared.

Liam was there instantly, enveloping her in a fierce, celebratory hug. "You were incredible, Pen! Absolutely incredible! Your voice was so clear, and your designs… oh my god, they just *spoke* to everyone!" His eyes, usually so focused on his camera, were now fixed on her, shining with unadulterated pride.

Her parents, their faces beaming, pushed through the small crowd gathering backstage. Her mother's eyes were glistening with unshed tears, her smile wide and tremulous. "My darling girl," she whispered, pulling Pennelopi into a warm embrace. "We are so, so proud of you." Her father, usually reserved, clapped her heartily on the back, a rare, beaming smile transforming his tired features. Even Leo, bouncing with uncontained excitement, declared, "You're the best fashion superhero ever, Pennelopi! Can I have the denim cape now?"

Pennelopi laughed, a genuine, unburdened sound that bubbled up from deep within her. The laughter felt liberating, a release of weeks of pent-up anxiety and self-doubt. The weight of shyness, which had always felt like a suffocating cloak, now seemed to have lifted, replaced by a lightness, a quiet confidence that settled comfortably within her. She was still Pennelopi, the girl with the glasses and the quiet demeanor, but something fundamental had shifted. She had found her voice, not by forcing herself to be someone she wasn't, but by speaking her truth, by letting her passion, her art, shine through.

As the immediate euphoria began to settle, Pennelopi's gaze drifted back to the runway. Other designers were presenting their collections, each one impressive in its own right. The plastic bottle dress, with its intricate LED lights, continued to draw gasps. The bicycle inner tube collection, with its industrial beat, maintained its edgy appeal. These were bold, high-concept pieces, undeniably professional, crafted from novel materials. But as

Pennelopi watched, she realized something profound. While those designs were visually striking, almost futuristic, hers offered something different. They offered warmth. They offered a story. They offered a connection to the past, reimagined for the future. They spoke of humanity, of resilience, of finding beauty in the overlooked.

The audience's reaction to her collection, though not immediately explosive like some of the more avant-garde pieces, had been one of quiet, sustained appreciation. There had been murmurs of "ingenious," "so creative," "I can't believe that's denim." People had leaned forward in their seats, their expressions shifting from polite curiosity to genuine fascination. It was a different kind of applause, perhaps, but one that felt deeply authentic.

Backstage, the atmosphere was a mix of nervous energy and celebratory relief. Designers hugged their models, photographers reviewed their shots, and volunteers began the slow process of clearing the runway. Pennelopi's models, Maya, Chloe, and Sarah, came back, their faces flushed with excitement.

"Everyone was talking about your phoenix dress, Pen!" Maya exclaimed, still glowing from her walk.

"They couldn't believe it was denim! And it was so comfortable!"

Chloe nodded enthusiastically. "And the jacket! People were trying to figure out how you made those flowers. It looked so cool!"

Sarah added, "My loungewear felt amazing. Like, I actually want to wear it every day. People were asking if they could buy it!"

Their genuine excitement was another balm to Pennelopi's soul. It wasn't just Mrs. Albright's validation; it was the models, the audience, the tangible proof that her vision had resonated.

As the main show concluded, the judges, including Mrs. Albright, gathered at a table set slightly apart from the main thoroughfare. Their heads were bent in serious deliberation, their clipboards filled with notes. Pennelopi watched them, a fresh wave of anticipation rising within her. The critiques were over. Now came the decision.

She couldn't hear their words, but she could imagine the debate. Mrs. Albright, with her sharp intellect and uncompromising standards, would undoubtedly be a formidable voice. Pennelopi remembered her initial, brutal assessment: *Naïve. Unrefined. Cumbersome. Jarring. Pedestrian. Patchwork.* But she also remembered Mrs. Albright's final words backstage, the subtle acknowledgment of her transformation, her newfound understanding of discipline and form. How would that translate in the judging room?

Pennelopi imagined Mrs. Albright, perhaps, defending her, not with effusive praise, but with precise, analytical arguments. "While Ms. Minyen's initial submission demonstrated a rudimentary understanding of drape and form, her subsequent revisions, particularly the nuanced integration of disparate materials and the sophisticated manipulation of texture, reveal a significant leap in mastery. The phoenix dress, once cumbersome, now exhibits a remarkable fluidity for denim. The Urban Bloom jacket, previously jarring, now achieves a harmonious dialogue between rigidity and organic growth. And the Comfort Reimagined loungewear, though deceptively simple, showcases an astute understanding of material properties and understated elegance. Her work demonstrates not just ingenuity in concept, but a rigorous application of learned principles. It speaks of a designer who listens, who learns, and who possesses the rare capacity for profound artistic evolution."

She could almost hear Mrs. Albright's gravelly voice, cutting through any superficial judgments, demanding that the other judges look beyond the "upcycled" label and see the true artistry. Pennelopi knew Mrs. Albright valued integrity and discipline above all else. And Pennelopi had certainly demonstrated both.

Meanwhile, the main hall was slowly transforming into a bustling community fair. Artisan stalls, which had been covered during the show, were now open, displaying their wares. People milled about, chatting, laughing, and, to Pennelopi's astonishment, many of them were still talking about her collection.

"Did you see that denim dress? I swear, it looked like it was floating!"

"And the jacket with the flowers! So clever, using old canvas like that."

"The loungewear, though. I would actually buy that. It looked so soft."

Pennelopi heard snippets of these conversations as she walked with Liam through the crowd, heading towards a quiet corner. A warmth spread through her chest. Her designs had resonated. They had sparked curiosity, admiration, and even a desire to own. This was a different kind of validation, a public acknowledgment that her "humble" creations had captivated the crowd.

As they navigated the throng, Liam suddenly nudged her. "Pen, look! It's her!"

Pennelopi followed his gaze. Standing near the entrance, chatting animatedly with a group of people, was a woman with vibrant pink hair, stylishly oversized glasses, and a brightly colored, avant-garde outfit. This was Celeste Dubois, a renowned fashion blogger and influencer known for her keen eye for emerging talent and her passionate advocacy for sustainable fashion. Her blog, "EcoChic Chronicles," was a major voice in the industry, and her reviews could make or break a young designer. Pennelopi had followed her blog for years, admiring her sharp critiques and her unwavering commitment to ethical fashion. The thought of Celeste Dubois seeing her work, let alone reviewing it, had been a distant, impossible dream.

Celeste was laughing, her hands gesturing expressively as she spoke. Then, her eyes, bright and intelligent, swept over the crowd, and for a moment, they landed on Pennelopi's display, still standing prominently near the runway. A flicker of interest crossed Celeste's face. She excused herself from her group and began to walk towards Pennelopi's collection, her pace quickening.

Pennelopi's heart began to pound anew. This wasn't the formal judging, but it felt even more significant. Celeste Dubois was the voice of the sustainable fashion movement. Her opinion mattered.

Celeste stopped in front of the phoenix dress, her head tilted, her expression thoughtful. She reached out, her fingers hovering just above the denim, as if reluctant to disturb its delicate flow. She then moved to the Urban Bloom jacket, examining the fabric flowers with a discerning eye. She spent a long time at each piece, her gaze intense, her lips occasionally forming a silent "wow."

Pennelopi watched, holding her breath. Liam, ever the professional, had subtly raised his camera, capturing the moment.

Finally, Celeste Dubois turned, her eyes sweeping over the hall, as if searching for someone. Her gaze landed on Pennelopi. A wide, genuine smile broke across her face.

She walked directly towards Pennelopi, her steps purposeful. Pennelopi felt her cheeks flush, her old shyness threatening to reassert itself. But then she remembered Mrs. Albright's words: *Stand tall. Your work deserves it.* She straightened her shoulders, meeting Celeste's gaze.

"Pennelopi Minyen?" Celeste asked, her voice vibrant and enthusiastic.

"Yes, ma'am," Pennelopi managed, her voice a little shaky.

Celeste's smile widened. "Ma'am? Please, call me Celeste! And 'ma'am' is far too formal for someone who just created *that.*" She gestured back at Pennelopi's collection. "Your collection, 'The Upcycled Dream' – it's absolutely breathtaking. Truly."

Pennelopi felt a wave of warmth spread through her. Celeste Dubois, the Celeste Dubois, was praising her work. Genuinely.

"I've seen a lot of upcycled fashion," Celeste continued, her eyes alight with genuine admiration, "but yours… yours is different. It's not just about repurposing; it's about reimagining. The phoenix dress, the way you made that denim flow, it's genius. And the lace, it's exquisite. It tells a story. And the Urban Bloom jacket – the way those flowers emerge from the canvas, it's so powerful. And the loungewear! So chic, so unexpected. You've taken discarded materials and elevated them into true art. You've found the soul in the discarded."

Pennelopi could only nod, overwhelmed. This was more than she could have ever dreamed of.

"I'm writing about this," Celeste declared, pulling out her phone. "I'm going to feature your collection prominently on EcoChic Chronicles. I need more photos. And I need to interview you. Right now, if you have a moment?"

Pennelopi's mind raced. An interview? With Celeste Dubois? Her shyness screamed in protest, but the thrill of the opportunity, the validation of her work, was stronger. "Yes," she managed, her voice gaining strength. "Yes, I'd love to."

Liam, ever the professional, stepped forward. "I have some high-resolution photos of the pieces, Celeste. And I'd be happy to take more for your feature."

Celeste's eyes lit up. "Perfect! This is going to be huge. Your work, Pennelopi, is exactly what the fashion world needs right now. It's not just sustainable; it's inspiring. It proves that true style isn't about money; it's about ingenuity and passion."

They found a quieter corner, and Pennelopi, with Liam's supportive presence beside her, found herself speaking with a surprising ease. She talked about her journey, about her family's financial struggles, about her love for discarded fabrics, about Mrs. Albright's mentorship, about the philosophy behind "The Upcycled Dream." She spoke with a quiet passion that transcended her lingering shyness, her words flowing freely as she articulated her artistic vision. Celeste listened intently, nodding, scribbling notes, her eyes sparkling with enthusiasm. Liam captured every moment, his camera a silent witness to Pennelopi's burgeoning success.

The interview concluded, and Celeste, after exchanging contact information with Pennelopi and Liam, hurried off, already tapping away on her phone, undoubtedly drafting her viral post.

Pennelopi felt lightheaded, a dizzying mix of exhaustion and exhilaration. She had just been interviewed by Celeste Dubois. Her work was going to be featured on EcoChic Chronicles. It was almost too much to process.

"That was amazing, Pen," Liam said, his voice full of awe. "She's going to make you famous!"

Pennelopi laughed, a little nervously. "Famous? I just want people to see that upcycling is more than just a trend. It's art."

The awards ceremony began shortly after. The announcer, a local radio personality, took to the stage, his voice booming. Pennelopi stood with her parents and Liam, her heart pounding with a fresh wave of nerves. She had already received such incredible validation; winning felt almost secondary.

The bronze and silver awards were announced for various categories. Then came the "Upcycled Design" category.

"And the bronze award for Upcycled Design goes to… the 'Plastic Bottle Gown' by Sarah Jenkins!" Polite applause.

"The silver award for Upcycled Design goes to… the 'Industrial Canvas Collection' by Marcus Thorne!" More applause.

Pennelopi felt a pang of disappointment, a small, familiar ache. She hadn't won. But then, she reminded herself, she had already won so much. She had presented her work, she had spoken, and Celeste Dubois had praised her. That was enough.

"And the gold award for Upcycled Design," the announcer's voice boomed, building to a dramatic crescendo, "goes to… 'The Upcycled Dream' collection by Pennelopi Minyen!"

For a moment, Pennelopi didn't move. She couldn't believe it. Her name. Her collection. Gold. Liam let out a whoop, pulling her into another hug. Her parents cheered, her mother openly weeping tears of joy.

"Go on, Pen!" Liam urged, gently pushing her towards the stage.

Pennelopi walked onto the stage in a daze, the applause a deafening roar. She accepted the small, eco-friendly trophy, her hands trembling slightly. She looked out at the audience, their faces a sea of smiling, cheering figures. She saw Liam, beaming. She saw her parents, their faces etched with pride. And then, her gaze found Mrs. Albright. The art teacher was standing, her hands clasped in front of her, a faint, almost imperceptible smile touching her lips. Her eyes, however, were not just proud; they held a deep, knowing satisfaction. A silent acknowledgment of a student who had not just learned, but had truly blossomed.

The next few days were a whirlwind. Celeste Dubois's blog post, "The Upcycled Dream: A Vision of Sustainable Genius," went viral. Her stunning photos of Pennelopi's collection, taken by Liam, were shared across social media platforms, garnering thousands of likes and comments. Fashion forums buzzed with discussions about Pennelopi's innovative use of materials, her unique aesthetic, and her powerful message. Major online fashion publications picked up the story, hailing Pennelopi as a "new voice" in sustainable design.

Pennelopi's phone, usually quiet, now buzzed incessantly with notifications. Emails poured in, requests for interviews, collaborations, and even inquiries about purchasing her designs. It was overwhelming, exhilarating, and utterly surreal. Her quiet, fabric-filled world had suddenly exploded onto the global stage.

One afternoon, a particularly official-looking email landed in her inbox. The subject line read: "Invitation: New York Fashion Week - Emerging Designers Showcase."

Pennelopi stared at it, her heart pounding. New York Fashion Week. The distant, shimmering mirage of her childhood dreams. It couldn't be real.

She opened the email, her hands trembling. It was from a scout for an independent showcase dedicated to emerging designers during New York Fashion Week. They had seen Celeste Dubois's feature on EcoChic Chronicles, had been captivated by Pennelopi's unique vision and sustainable approach, and were extending an unbelievable invitation: a special, independent showcase for emerging designers, a chance to present her collection on one of the most prestigious fashion stages in the world.

Pennelopi read the email three times, then again. She ran to Liam's house, the email still open on her phone.

"Liam! Look at this! I don't… I don't understand. Is this real?" she stammered, thrusting the phone into his hands.

Liam read it, his eyes widening with each line. His jaw dropped. "Holy smokes, Pen! This is… this is it! New York Fashion Week! This is your big break! This is absolutely real!" He pulled her into another ecstatic hug, spinning her around.

Pennelopi felt a dizzying mix of disbelief and exhilaration. Her upcycled dream, once a quiet whisper in her bedroom, was now roaring to life, pulling her towards the glittering lights of New York. It was terrifying, exhilarating, and utterly unbelievable. She, Pennelopi Minyen, the shy teen with glasses, was going to New York Fashion Week. The vision had been unveiled, and the world was taking notice. The threads of her dream were now weaving into a tapestry far grander than she could have ever imagined.

Chapter 8: The Unexpected Invitation

The email, stark white against the glowing screen of her phone, seemed to vibrate with an impossible energy. "Invitation: New York Fashion Week - Emerging Designers Showcase." Pennelopi stared at the words, her breath caught in her throat, her mind struggling to reconcile the mundane reality of her small bedroom with the glittering, distant mirage of her wildest dreams. New York Fashion Week. It was a place she had only ever visited in the glossy pages of magazines, a hallowed ground for fashion titans, not for a shy teen from a small town who made art from discarded clothes.

"Liam! Look at this! I don't… I don't understand. Is this real?" she stammered, thrusting her phone into his hands. She had run to his house, the email still open, the words burning themselves into her retina. Her heart hammered against her ribs, a frantic, joyous drumbeat.

Liam's eyes, usually so calm and observant, widened with each line he read. His jaw dropped, and a slow, incredulous grin spread across his face. "Holy smokes, Pen! This is… this is it! New York Fashion Week! This is your big break! This is absolutely real!"

He whooped, a loud, uninhibited sound, and pulled her into another ecstatic hug, spinning her around until the room blurred.

Pennelopi felt a dizzying mix of disbelief and exhilaration. Her upcycled dream, once a quiet whisper in her bedroom, was now roaring to life, pulling her towards the glittering lights of New York. It was terrifying, exhilarating, and utterly unbelievable. She, Pennelopi Minyen, the shy teen with glasses, was going to New York Fashion Week. The vision had been unveiled, and the world was taking notice. The threads of her dream were now weaving into a tapestry far grander than she could have ever imagined.

They spent the next hour re-reading the email, dissecting every word, every clause. It was an invitation to a special, independent showcase for emerging designers, held concurrently with the main Fashion Week events. It wasn't the main stage, not yet, but it was *there*. It was a foot in the door, an unprecedented opportunity. The scout had seen Celeste Dubois's feature on "EcoChic Chronicles," had been captivated by Pennelopi's unique vision and sustainable approach, and believed her work embodied the future of fashion.

"We have to tell your parents!" Liam finally exclaimed, breaking the spell of their shared disbelief. "This is huge, Pen! This changes everything!"

Pennelopi nodded, a nervous flutter returning to her stomach. Telling her parents felt like making it truly real, truly tangible. They were supportive, yes, but they also understood the harsh realities of their financial situation. New York, even for a showcase, would undoubtedly involve costs. Travel, accommodation, additional materials for new pieces – it all added up.

They rushed back to Pennelopi's house, bursting through the door, their excitement barely contained. Her parents were in the living room, her mother knitting, her father reading the newspaper. Leo was sprawled on the floor, drawing.

"Mom! Dad! You won't believe it!" Pennelopi blurted out, her voice high with excitement, thrusting the phone at them before Liam could even get a word in.

Her mother took the phone, her brow furrowing as she read the email. Her eyes widened, then she looked up at Pennelopi, her expression a mixture of awe and concern. Her father, sensing the unusual urgency, put down his newspaper and leaned forward.

"New York Fashion Week?" her mother whispered, her voice barely audible. "Pennelopi, is this… is this real?"

"Yes, Mom! It's real! It's an invitation to a showcase for emerging designers!" Pennelopi explained, her words tumbling out in a rush. "They saw Celeste Dubois's blog post, and they want me to show my collection!"

Her father took the phone, reading the email carefully. He looked up at Pennelopi, a slow, proud smile spreading across his face. "Our Pennelopi. New York Fashion Week. Who would have thought?" His voice was thick with emotion.

But then, the practical questions began. "Honey, New York is expensive," her mother said, her voice tinged with worry. "Travel, a place to stay… and you'd need to expand your collection, wouldn't you? More designs?"

Pennelopi nodded, the excitement tempered by the sudden return of financial reality. "Yes, I would need to create a whole new mini-collection, probably five or six more pieces. And the travel… I know it's a lot."

A silence fell over the room, heavy with the weight of their family's financial constraints. Pennelopi watched her parents, her heart sinking. She knew how hard they worked, how carefully they budgeted. Was this dream, this incredible opportunity, simply too much of a burden?

Then, her father cleared his throat. "Pennelopi," he said, his voice firm, "this is a once-in-a-lifetime opportunity. Your talent, your hard work… you deserve this. We'll find a way." He looked at her mother, who nodded, her eyes still worried, but resolute. "We'll make it work. We'll figure it out. This is your dream, honey. We're behind you, all the way."

Leo, sensing the momentousness of the occasion, jumped up and hugged Pennelopi's leg. "You're going to be famous, Pennelopi! And then you can buy me a real superhero cape!"

Pennelopi felt tears prick her eyes, but this time, they were tears of overwhelming gratitude and love. Her family, despite their struggles, was willing to make sacrifices for her dream. It filled her with a fierce determination to make them proud, to make every penny, every effort, worth it.

The next day, Pennelopi called Mrs. Albright. She recounted the entire story, from Celeste Dubois's blog post to the New York Fashion Week invitation.

She half-expected Mrs. Albright to dismiss it as a fleeting moment of hype, another example of the superficiality of the fashion world.

Instead, Mrs. Albright listened intently, her silence more attentive than any exclamation. When Pennelopi finished, there was a long pause.

"New York Fashion Week," Mrs. Albright finally stated, her voice a low, thoughtful murmur. "A significant platform, Ms. Minyen. A crucible. It will test your resolve, your artistry, and your understanding of the industry's demands. Are you prepared for that level of scrutiny?"

"I... I think so, ma'am," Pennelopi replied, her voice a little shaky. "I want to be. I want to show what upcycling can really be."

"Good," Mrs. Albright said, a rare note of approval in her voice. "Because this is not merely about creating pretty garments, Ms. Minyen. This is about making a statement. About defining your voice on a grander stage. Your 'Upcycled Dream' must resonate with a wider audience, with an industry often resistant to change. It must be impeccable. It must be unforgettable."

She then shifted gears, her voice becoming brisk and practical. "You will need to expand your collection.

Not just more pieces, but pieces that demonstrate a broader range of your capabilities, while maintaining a cohesive narrative. We will meet every day after school. Your existing collection, while strong, was designed for a local fair. New York demands a different level of polish, a different kind of impact. We will refine. We will innovate. We will push the boundaries of what is possible with upcycled materials."

The mentorship intensified, becoming a whirlwind of creative intensity. Mrs. Albright, usually so reserved, seemed to come alive with a new fervor, her eyes sparkling with intellectual challenge. She pushed Pennelopi harder than ever before, demanding not just technical excellence, but conceptual depth, a profound understanding of the message she wanted to convey.

Their sessions in Room 307 became a rigorous design laboratory. Mrs. Albright made Pennelopi research current fashion trends, not to emulate them, but to understand the prevailing aesthetic and how her upcycled vision could offer a compelling alternative. They studied the work of avant-garde designers, analyzing how they pushed boundaries, how they challenged conventional notions of beauty and wearability.

"Your challenge, Ms. Minyen," Mrs. Albright explained one afternoon, sketching furiously in her notebook, "is to elevate upcycling beyond a mere novelty. It must be seen as a legitimate, even superior, form of design. It must be chic. It must be desirable. It must be *fashion.*"

Pennelopi's new mini-collection for New York began to take shape, guided by Mrs. Albright's exacting standards. She decided to expand on the themes of transformation and resilience, but with a more sophisticated, almost ethereal aesthetic. She wanted to showcase the versatility of upcycled materials, proving they could be luxurious, elegant, and utterly modern.

One of the new pieces she envisioned was a "Deconstructed Evening Gown," a formal dress crafted from discarded silk scarves and vintage lace curtains. Mrs. Albright challenged her to create a gown that flowed with the fluidity of water, its patchwork almost invisible, its textures seamlessly integrated. This required Pennelopi to master intricate draping techniques, to understand how to manipulate sheer fabrics, and to develop an almost invisible stitching method. She spent hours meticulously hand-stitching the delicate silk, ensuring each seam was perfectly aligned, each piece of lace integrated with artistic precision.

Another concept was a "Sculptural Outerwear" piece, a coat or jacket made from repurposed wool blankets and felted sweaters. Mrs. Albright pushed her to create a garment with dramatic volume and architectural lines, yet one that retained the inherent warmth and comfort of the original materials. This involved experimenting with felting techniques, layering different weights of wool, and developing innovative pattern-making approaches to create structural integrity without excessive bulk. Pennelopi learned to use the inherent stiffness of felted wool to create dramatic collars and cuffs, while the softer, draped sections provided comfort and movement.

The third new piece was a "Transformed Accessories" line, focusing on handbags and statement jewelry made from discarded leather scraps, metal hardware, and even old electronic components. Mrs. Albright emphasized the importance of cohesive styling, showing how accessories could elevate an entire collection, providing a narrative link between the garments. Pennelopi found herself researching industrial design, studying the mechanics of clasps and hinges, and experimenting with unconventional materials like salvaged circuit boards and copper wire, transforming them into surprisingly elegant and edgy adornments.

The financial hurdles were a constant, low hum beneath the surface of their excitement. Her parents, true to their word, began to make sacrifices. Her father took on extra shifts, his already tired eyes growing even more weary. Her mother started selling some of her knitted goods at local craft fairs, pouring every extra dollar into Pennelopi's "New York Fund." They even had a small, quiet family meeting where they discussed cutting back on non-essentials – no more takeout, stricter limits on electricity, even postponing a much-needed repair on the family car. Pennelopi felt a profound sense of responsibility, a silent pressure to make every sacrifice count, to prove that their belief in her was not misplaced.

Liam, meanwhile, became her unofficial publicist and creative director. He meticulously documented every step of her design process, capturing the raw materials, the deconstruction, the painstaking reassembly. His photographs, already professional-quality, became even more refined, anticipating the high standards of the fashion industry. He started building a digital portfolio for Pennelopi, showcasing her journey and her unique aesthetic. He also took on the role of managing her burgeoning online presence, responding to inquiries, and filtering out the less serious requests, allowing Pennelopi to focus entirely on her designs.

"You need to start thinking about the story you'll tell in New York, Pen," Liam reminded her one evening, as she worked late into the night on a particularly challenging seam. "It's not just about the clothes; it's about the narrative. Your narrative. The upcycled dream, but on a global scale."

Pennelopi nodded, her mind already buzzing with ideas. She wanted to convey the message that sustainability wasn't a compromise, but an opportunity for unparalleled creativity and innovation. She wanted to show that beauty could be found in the most unexpected places, that discarded materials held immense potential, and that true style was a reflection of ingenuity and conscious choice.

The pressure mounted with each passing day. The deadlines were tight, the expectations immense. Pennelopi found herself working late into the night, fueled by strong coffee and an unshakeable determination. Her fingers ached, her eyes burned, but the vision of her designs on a New York runway, the dream of proving her worth on the grandest stage, kept her going.

Her shyness, though significantly diminished, still resurfaced in moments of extreme stress. She'd find herself rehearsing her presentation in front of the mirror, her voice faltering, her hands trembling. But then she'd remember Mrs. Albright's piercing gaze, her demand for discipline, her belief in Pennelopi's inherent talent. She'd remember Liam's unwavering support, her parents' sacrifices. And she'd push through. She learned to channel her nervous energy into focused concentration, transforming anxiety into meticulous precision.

The first interaction with the New York Fashion Week organizers was a nerve-wracking experience. It was a video call with a stern-faced woman named Ms. Davies, the head of the Emerging Designers Showcase. Ms. Davies spoke in clipped, efficient tones, outlining the rigorous schedule, the technical requirements for the runway, and the demanding expectations for the designers. She reviewed Pennelopi's initial sketches and the photos Liam had sent, her expression unreadable.

"Your concept is compelling, Ms. Minyen," Ms. Davies stated, her voice devoid of warmth. "And your initial collection shows promise. However, New

York Fashion Week is a different league. The industry demands perfection. Flawless execution. Are you confident you can meet these standards?"

Pennelopi took a deep breath, remembering Mrs. Albright's lessons on standing tall, on articulating her vision with conviction. "Yes, Ms. Davies," she replied, her voice firm, surprising even herself. "I am confident. My mentor, Mrs. Albright, has instilled in me the discipline and understanding required for this level of precision. And my collection will not only meet, but exceed, expectations for innovation and craftsmanship, while staying true to the sustainable ethos of 'The Upcycled Dream.'"

Ms. Davies's expression remained impassive, but Pennelopi thought she detected a faint flicker of something in her eyes – perhaps a hint of surprise, or even grudging respect. "Very well, Ms. Minyen. We look forward to seeing your completed collection. The runway schedule and final submission details will be sent to you next week. Do not disappoint."

The call ended, and Pennelopi collapsed back in her chair, a shaky laugh escaping her lips. She had done it. She had faced the formidable Ms. Davies, and she hadn't crumbled. She had stood her ground, articulated her vision, and projected a confidence she was only just beginning to truly feel.

The surreal nature of it all began to sink in. She was really going. The plane tickets were booked, a small, affordable Airbnb secured for her and Liam, thanks to her parents' relentless saving and a small, anonymous donation that Mrs. Albright had subtly facilitated through a school art fund. Her passport, once a dusty relic, was now a symbol of her impending journey.

Her room, once a private haven, was now a bustling design studio, a testament to her relentless work. Finished pieces for the New York collection hung on a new, sturdier rack, their fabrics shimmering under the work lights. The deconstructed evening gown, a cascade of repurposed silk and lace, flowed with an almost liquid grace. The sculptural outerwear, a dramatic silhouette crafted from felted wool, exuded an unexpected elegance. The transformed accessories, edgy and chic, completed the narrative. Each piece was a testament to her growth, to Mrs. Albright's demanding but transformative mentorship, and to her own unwavering dedication.

One last evening before their departure, Pennelopi stood in her room, looking at her finished collection.

The phoenix dress, the Urban Bloom jacket, the Comfort Reimagined loungewear, and the new additions – all of them spoke of her journey, of the discarded transformed into the magnificent. She ran her fingers over the rich textures, feeling the history embedded in each thread, the promise of a new future.

Her parents came in, their faces tired but filled with a quiet pride. Her mother gently adjusted a fold on the evening gown. "It's beautiful, Pennelopi," she whispered, her voice thick with emotion. "Absolutely beautiful."

Her father put an arm around her shoulder. "You worked so hard for this, honey. You deserve every bit of it."

Leo, already in his pajamas, wandered in, rubbing sleep from his eyes. He looked at the dresses, then at Pennelopi. "Are you really going to New York, Pennelopi? To the big fashion show?"

Pennelopi knelt down, pulling him into a hug. "Yes, Leo. I am. And I'm going to show them that old clothes can be amazing."

He grinned. "Cool! Don't forget my cape!"

Pennelopi laughed, a genuine, happy sound. The fear of the big city, the immense pressure of Fashion

Week, still lingered, a faint hum beneath the surface. But it was overshadowed by a profound sense of purpose, a deep gratitude, and an unshakeable belief in her upcycled dream. The journey to New York was not just a physical one; it was a journey of self-discovery, of artistic evolution, of a shy girl finding her voice on the grandest stage imaginable. The unexpected invitation had been received, and Pennelopi Minyen, the young designer with glasses, was ready to answer the call.

Chapter 9: Stepping into the Spotlight

The hum of the airplane engines was a low, resonant thrum beneath Pennelopi's seat, a sound that vibrated through her bones and echoed the frantic beat of her heart. Below, the patchwork quilt of familiar farmlands and small towns slowly gave way to the sprawling, intricate web of urban sprawl, a concrete tapestry stretching endlessly towards the horizon. New York. The very name felt like a whispered promise, a dazzling, terrifying reality.

Liam, seated beside her, was already meticulously reviewing the photos on his camera, his brow furrowed in concentration. He had insisted on capturing every moment of their journey, from the nervous farewells at the tiny local airport to the fleeting glimpses of clouds outside the plane window. His calm, focused presence was a comforting anchor in the whirlwind of Pennelopi's emotions.

"Almost there, Pen," he murmured, sensing her quiet intensity. "You ready for the big city?"

Pennelopi managed a shaky smile. "As ready as I'll ever be. It still feels… unreal." She adjusted her glasses, pushing them higher on her nose. The worn frames, once a symbol of her shyness, now felt like a familiar shield, a small piece of home amidst the overwhelming newness.

The flight had been booked with painstaking care, choosing the most economical option, a testament to her parents' sacrifices. Every dollar counted, every expense was weighed. The small, anonymous donation from Mrs. Albright, subtly channeled through a school art fund, had been a crucial lifeline, covering their modest Airbnb and some essential supplies. Pennelopi felt the weight of their collective effort, a silent pressure to make every moment in New York count, to prove that their belief in her was not misplaced.

Landing at JFK was an assault on the senses. The air, thick with the exhaust of countless vehicles, felt different, sharper. The roar of traffic, the cacophony of a thousand conversations, the blur of faces rushing past – it was a sensory overload, a stark contrast to the quiet, predictable rhythms of her small town. Pennelopi felt a familiar tightening in her chest, the old shyness threatening to reassert itself amidst the overwhelming anonymity of the city. She clung to Liam's arm, her knuckles white.

"Just breathe, Pen," Liam said, his voice calm amidst the chaos. "It's a lot, but you'll get used to it. Think of it as a giant, living canvas."

Their Airbnb was in a quiet, tree-lined street in Brooklyn, a small, cozy apartment that offered a much-needed respite from the city's relentless energy. It was modest, but clean and functional, a stark contrast to the luxurious hotels where many of the established designers would be staying. Pennelopi didn't care. All she needed was a space to work, a quiet corner to prepare her collection for the grand stage.

The first few days in New York were a whirlwind of logistics and nervous anticipation. They navigated the subway, a bewildering labyrinth of screeching trains and bustling platforms, learning to read the complex map and decipher the rapid-fire announcements. They visited the venue for the Emerging Designers Showcase – a repurposed industrial loft in Chelsea, its exposed brick and high ceilings providing a raw, edgy backdrop for the runway. It was smaller than the main Fashion Week tents, but it still felt immense, intimidating.

Pennelopi met Ms. Davies in person. The head of the showcase was as stern and efficient as she had been on the video call, her gaze piercing, her expectations clearly articulated. "Ms. Minyen," Ms. Davies stated, her voice clipped, "your collection must be flawless. Every stitch, every detail. We are showcasing the future of fashion. There is no room for error." She walked through Pennelopi's initial pieces, her expression unreadable, offering no praise, only a silent, intense scrutiny. Pennelopi felt the pressure mount, a heavy weight settling on her shoulders.

Back at the Airbnb, Pennelopi plunged into the final preparations for her collection. Her small living room transformed into a temporary design studio, fabric scraps once again blooming around her, though this time, they were the precious remnants of her carefully curated upcycled materials. The "Deconstructed Evening Gown," a cascade of repurposed silk scarves and vintage lace curtains, hung on a makeshift rack, its delicate beauty shimmering under the apartment lights. The "Sculptural Outerwear" piece, a dramatic coat crafted from felted wool blankets, stood sentinel on a borrowed mannequin, its architectural lines commanding attention. The "Transformed Accessories," edgy and chic, lay meticulously arranged on a small table.

The pressure was immense. New York Fashion Week was a different beast entirely from the local "Green Stitch" show. Here, the competition was fierce, the stakes higher, the eyes of the industry far more discerning. Pennelopi found herself obsessing over every detail, re-checking seams, re-pressing fabrics, convinced that any tiny imperfection would be magnified under the harsh glare of the professional runway lights. She wanted her collection to be perfect, not just for the judges, but for herself, a tangible proof that she had truly overcome her limitations and was worthy of this grand stage.

She worked late into the nights, fueled by strong coffee and an unshakeable determination. Her fingers ached, her eyes burned, but the vision of her designs on a New York runway, the dream of proving her worth on the grandest stage, kept her going. She remembered Mrs. Albright's words: *Your 'Upcycled Dream' must resonate with a wider audience, with an industry often resistant to change. It must be impeccable. It must be unforgettable.*

Liam, ever her steadfast support, was a constant presence. He helped her organize her materials, ran errands for last-minute supplies, and, most importantly, provided a calm, reassuring presence amidst the mounting stress. He meticulously documented every step of her preparation, his camera clicking softly as he captured the intricate details of her work, the focused intensity in her eyes. He was building a visual narrative of her journey, a testament to her dedication and talent.

"You're doing great, Pen," he'd say, watching her meticulously hand-stitch a delicate detail onto the evening gown. "Every stitch is perfect. This is going to blow them away."

But even Liam's unwavering belief couldn't entirely quell the internal turmoil. Her shyness, though significantly diminished, still resurfaced in moments of extreme stress. She'd find herself rehearsing her presentation in front of the mirror, her voice faltering, her hands trembling. The thought of facing a room full of jaded fashion critics, of having to articulate her vision to an audience that might be skeptical of "upcycled" fashion, was terrifying.

She called Mrs. Albright frequently, seeking solace and guidance. Mrs. Albright, despite the distance, remained her unwavering mentor. Her voice, gravelly and precise over the phone, was a grounding force.

"Ms. Minyen," Mrs. Albright would say, her tone devoid of sentimentality but rich with wisdom, "pressure is a privilege. It means your work is being seen, being challenged. Do not succumb to the superficiality of perfection. Focus on the integrity of your vision. Your designs are not merely clothes; they are a philosophy. Let that philosophy guide your hand, and your voice."

One evening, Pennelopi was particularly overwhelmed. A seam on the sculptural coat refused to lie flat, and a sudden wave of self-doubt washed over her. She called Mrs. Albright, her voice thick with frustration.

"It's just… it feels like it's not good enough," Pennelopi confessed, tears pricking her eyes. "Everything has to be so perfect, and I'm just… me. A girl from a small town, with old fabrics."

There was a long pause on the other end of the line. Then, Mrs. Albright's voice, softer than usual, broke the silence. "Ms. Minyen, perfection is an illusion. Integrity is the foundation of true art. Your 'old fabrics,' as you call them, carry a history, a soul. That is your strength. That is your unique voice. Do not try to be someone you are not. Do not try to emulate the established. They have their voice. You have yours. And your voice, Ms. Minyen, is one the world needs to hear."

She paused, then added, "Remember the lessons of the muslin. The language of materials. The flow of form. Trust your hands. Trust your eye. And trust the journey that brought you to this moment. You are not 'just a girl from a small town.' You are a designer of remarkable ingenuity and passion. Stand by that. Believe in that."

Mrs. Albright's words were a powerful balm to Pennelopi's soul. They reminded her of the core of her artistry, the philosophy that had always driven her. It wasn't about being flawless in the conventional sense; it was about being true to her vision, to the story she wanted to tell. The conversation was a crucial turning point, allowing Pennelopi to release the suffocating pressure of external expectations and reconnect with her inner artistic conviction.

The days leading up to the showcase were a blur of fittings with the professional models provided by the showcase organizers. These models were different from her school friends – tall, poised, with an almost ethereal grace. Pennelopi, usually intimidated by new social interactions, found herself surprisingly at ease. She communicated her vision clearly, explaining the nuances of each garment, the way the fabric should flow, the attitude each piece conveyed. She saw her designs come alive on their bodies, transformed from static creations into dynamic, wearable art.

Liam, meanwhile, was tirelessly working on Pennelopi's digital presence. He created a sleek, professional website showcasing her collection, complete with his stunning photographs and a compelling narrative about "The Upcycled Dream." He managed her social media, responding to inquiries from fashion enthusiasts and media outlets, ensuring that Pennelopi's unique story reached a wider audience. He even secured a few pre-show interviews with smaller online fashion publications, giving Pennelopi valuable practice in articulating her vision to the press.

One afternoon, during a break from fittings, Pennelopi found herself being interviewed by a young journalist from an online sustainable fashion magazine. The journalist, earnest and enthusiastic, asked about her inspirations, her process, her message. Pennelopi, surprisingly, found herself speaking with ease, her voice clear and passionate. She talked about the beauty of discarded materials, the importance of conscious consumption, the power of creativity to transform not just fabric, but perspectives.

"For me," Pennelopi explained, her eyes alight with conviction, "upcycling isn't just a trend. It's a philosophy. It's about seeing potential where others see waste. It's about giving a second life to materials, reducing our environmental footprint, and proving that luxury and elegance don't have to come at the expense of the planet. Every piece in 'The Upcycled Dream' collection tells a story of transformation, of resilience, of finding beauty in the unexpected."

The journalist nodded, scribbling furiously. "That's a powerful message, Pennelopi. And your designs truly embody it. They're breathtaking."

The interview was a small triumph, a confirmation that her voice, once so timid, was now capable of resonating with others, of conveying the profound message behind her art. It was a testament to her personal growth, to her ability to overcome her shyness and stand up for her artistic vision.

As the day of the Emerging Designers Showcase dawned, Pennelopi felt a mix of nerves and exhilaration. The loft venue in Chelsea was buzzing with activity. Backstage, the atmosphere was a controlled chaos of hair and makeup artists, models, and designers making last-minute adjustments. The air was thick with the scent of hairspray and the nervous energy of anticipation.

Pennelopi's section was meticulously organized, her collection hanging perfectly, each piece ready for its moment in the spotlight. She looked at the

"Deconstructed Evening Gown," its silk shimmering, its lace intricate. She looked at the "Sculptural Outerwear," its wool felted into dramatic forms. She looked at the "Transformed Accessories," their unexpected materials transformed into elegant adornments. They were impeccable. They were unforgettable. They were her upcycled dream, brought to life on the grandest stage.

She saw Ms. Davies moving through the backstage area, her expression as stern as ever, but Pennelopi no longer felt intimidated. She had met Ms. Davies's challenge, and she had delivered.

Her models, dressed and ready, lined up at the entrance to the runway. Pennelopi gave them a final pep talk, her voice calm and encouraging. "Just remember the story of each piece," she told them. "Let the clothes speak. And walk with confidence. You are embodying a dream."

As the lights dimmed and the music swelled, Pennelopi felt a surge of adrenaline. This was it. The culmination of years of quiet dreaming, months of rigorous training, and weeks of intense preparation. This was her moment.

The first model, wearing the "Deconstructed Evening Gown," stepped onto the runway. The silk flowed like water, the lace shimmering under the lights. The audience, a mix of fashion critics, industry insiders, and curious enthusiasts, murmured with appreciation. Pennelopi watched, her heart pounding, but this time, it was a rhythm of excitement, not fear.

The models walked with grace and poise, showcasing each piece of Pennelopi's collection. The "Sculptural Outerwear" commanded attention with its dramatic silhouette. The "Transformed Accessories" added an unexpected edge, proving that sustainable design could be both elegant and avant-garde. The original pieces from the "Green Stitch" show – the phoenix dress, the Urban Bloom jacket, the Comfort Reimagined loungewear – now appeared with a new level of polish, their inherent beauty amplified by Pennelopi's refined craftsmanship.

The audience's reaction was palpable. There were gasps, whispers, and then, a growing wave of applause. Pennelopi saw heads nodding, phones being raised to capture images, and a few fashion critics scribbling furiously in their notebooks. Her unique vision, her powerful message, her impeccable craftsmanship – it was all resonating.

As the final model exited the runway, the applause swelled into a thunderous ovation, a roar of approval that filled the loft. Pennelopi felt a profound sense of accomplishment, a quiet triumph that settled deep within her. She had come to New York, a shy girl with a dream, and she had unveiled a vision that captivated an industry.

She stepped onto the runway for her final bow, the spotlight blinding, the applause deafening. She stood tall, her shoulders back, a quiet smile touching her lips. She looked out at the sea of faces, and for the first time, she truly saw herself not as a shy teen with glasses, but as Pennelopi Minyen, a designer with a powerful voice, a unique vision, and an upcycled dream that was finally stepping into the spotlight. The journey had been arduous, but every challenge, every doubt, every sacrifice had been worth it. This was just the beginning.

Chapter 10: The Youngest Star

The roar of applause that enveloped Pennelopi as she took her final bow on the Chelsea loft runway was a sound unlike anything she had ever experienced. It wasn't just a polite acknowledgment; it was a visceral, thunderous ovation that vibrated through the very floorboards, through her bones, through the core of her being. The spotlight, once a blinding interrogator, now felt like a warm embrace, illuminating not just her, but the culmination of years of quiet dreaming, months of rigorous training, and weeks of intense, often overwhelming, preparation. She stood tall, her shoulders back, a quiet, genuine smile touching her lips. In that moment, the cacophony of the city, the pressure of Fashion Week, the lingering whispers of her shyness – all faded into a distant hum, replaced by the profound, exhilarating certainty that she had done it. She had unveiled her vision, and it had resonated.

As she walked off the runway, the applause still ringing in her ears, Liam was there, his face alight with unadulterated joy. He pulled her into a triumphant hug, his camera, for once, forgotten. "You were incredible, Pen! Absolutely incredible! They loved it! You could feel it, right?"

Pennelopi could only nod, a breathless laugh escaping her lips. Her eyes, still adjusting from the glare of the spotlight, scanned the faces of the backstage crew and the other designers. There were smiles, nods of congratulations, even a few murmurs of "amazing" and "genius." The atmosphere was electric, charged with the lingering energy of a successful show.

Ms. Davies, the stern head of the Emerging Designers Showcase, approached them. Her expression, usually so unreadable, held a flicker of something akin to impressed satisfaction. "Ms. Minyen," she stated, her voice still clipped, but with a new undertone of respect, "your collection was… compelling. It offered a fresh perspective. You exceeded expectations." She gave a curt nod, a rare gesture of approval from the formidable organizer, and then moved on, leaving Pennelopi feeling a surge of quiet triumph.

The immediate aftermath of the showcase was a controlled chaos of interviews, photographs, and networking. Journalists, who had been scribbling furiously in their notebooks during the show, now swarmed Pennelopi, their recorders thrust forward, their questions rapid-fire.

"Pennelopi, your use of upcycled materials is revolutionary! How do you achieve such fluidity with denim?"

"What inspired the architectural lines in your outerwear?"

"Your message of sustainability – how do you see it impacting the future of high fashion?"

Pennelopi, surprisingly, found herself answering with a newfound ease. The practice sessions with Liam, the intellectual rigor of Mrs. Albright's critiques, and the profound conviction in her own message had prepared her for this moment. She spoke with a quiet passion, articulating her design philosophy, explaining the technical challenges and creative solutions behind each piece. She talked about the history embedded in the discarded fabrics, the stories they carried, and the new narratives she sought to weave. Her voice, though still soft, was clear, confident, and resonated with an authentic sincerity that captivated the reporters.

Liam, meanwhile, was in his element. He moved through the crowd with professional grace, capturing every angle, every candid moment. He coordinated with journalists, ensured Pennelopi had water, and subtly steered her away from overly aggressive interviewers. He was her silent guardian, her strategic partner, and her most dedicated documentarian.

The buzz surrounding Pennelopi's collection began immediately. Social media exploded with images and videos from the showcase. Fashion bloggers, industry insiders, and environmental activists alike hailed her as a groundbreaking talent. Celeste Dubois's "EcoChic Chronicles" published an immediate follow-up post, gushing with praise: "Pennelopi Minyen: The Upcycled Visionary Who Just Redefined Luxury." Her stunning photos of Pennelopi's collection, captured by Liam, were shared thousands of times, becoming instant viral sensations.

The next morning, the reviews began to pour in. Major fashion publications, usually reserved in their praise for emerging designers, dedicated significant space to "The Upcycled Dream."

Vogue Online declared: "In a season often dominated by excess, Pennelopi Minyen's 'The Upcycled Dream' offered a refreshing, poignant counter-narrative. Her meticulous craftsmanship and profound understanding of material transformation elevate discarded fabrics into haute couture. A true visionary."

Fashion Daily wrote: "Minyen's collection is a masterclass in ingenuity. She proves that sustainability is not a compromise, but an opportunity for unparalleled creativity. Her 'phoenix dress,' a cascade of repurposed denim and lace, is a standout, a testament to her ability to find beauty in the unexpected."

The New York Times Style Section published a thoughtful piece, noting: "While the industry grapples with its environmental impact, Pennelopi Minyen, a young designer from an unassuming background, offers a compelling solution. Her 'Upcycled Dream' collection is not just aesthetically pleasing; it is a powerful statement about conscious consumption, resourcefulness, and the enduring power of human creativity. Her work challenges us to reconsider our notions of value and luxury."

Pennelopi read the reviews in their modest Airbnb, tears blurring her vision. It wasn't just the praise; it was the *understanding.* They saw her vision. They grasped her message. They recognized the years of quiet dedication, the lessons learned, the passion poured into every stitch.

Her phone, usually quiet, now buzzed incessantly with notifications – emails from major fashion houses, inquiries from high-end boutiques, requests for collaborations, and interview invitations from national television shows. It was overwhelming, exhilarating, and utterly surreal. Her quiet, fabric-filled world had suddenly exploded onto the global stage.

One afternoon, amidst the whirlwind of media attention, Pennelopi received a call that made her heart leap into her throat. It was from the official New York Fashion Week organizing committee. They wanted to meet with her. Immediately.

Liam accompanied her to the meeting, held in a sleek, glass-walled office high above the city. The committee members, a group of impeccably dressed, serious-faced individuals, greeted her with a new deference, a subtle shift in their demeanor that spoke volumes.

The lead committee member, a formidable woman with an air of quiet authority, began to speak. "Ms. Minyen," she said, her voice calm and measured, "your showcase at the Emerging Designers event has created an unprecedented stir. Your collection, 'The Upcycled Dream,' has resonated deeply with critics, industry leaders, and the public alike. It is not merely a collection; it is a movement."

Pennelopi listened, her heart pounding.

"The committee," the woman continued, "has made a unanimous decision. We believe your vision, your message, and your exceptional talent represent the future of American fashion. Therefore, we would like to extend an official invitation for you to present a full collection at the main New York Fashion Week runway next season. And," she paused, a faint smile touching her lips, "in recognition of your groundbreaking debut and the profound impact you have already made, we would like to formally acknowledge you as the youngest designer ever to officially show at New York Fashion Week."

Pennelopi felt the air leave her lungs. The youngest designer. Ever. It was a title that transcended her wildest dreams, a recognition that validated every sacrifice, every doubt, every single stitch. She looked at Liam, whose eyes were wide with disbelief and joy.

"Ms. Minyen?" the committee member prompted, sensing her stunned silence.

Pennelopi found her voice, a little shaky, but filled with profound gratitude. "Thank you," she whispered. "Thank you so much. This is… this is an incredible honor."

The news broke immediately. The official announcement from New York Fashion Week sent shockwaves through the industry. "Teen Visionary Pennelopi Minyen to Become Youngest Designer to Show at NYFW." The headlines were everywhere, plastered across fashion blogs, news sites, and social media. Pennelopi Minyen, the shy teen with glasses, was no longer just an emerging talent; she was a phenomenon.

The attention was dizzying. She was invited to appear on morning talk shows, interviewed by major newspapers, and featured in glossy fashion magazines. She found herself sitting in green rooms, surrounded by makeup artists and stylists, her mind still grappling with the surreal reality of it all. In every interview, she spoke with a quiet passion, her voice clear and articulate, advocating for sustainable fashion, for finding beauty in the overlooked, for the power of ingenuity and conscious choice. She never forgot her roots, always crediting her family's support, Liam's unwavering belief, and Mrs. Albright's uncompromising mentorship.

"My journey began out of necessity," she explained in one interview, her eyes shining with conviction. "My family couldn't afford expensive materials, so I found beauty in discarded fabrics. But it quickly became more than just necessity; it became a philosophy. Every piece I create tells a story of transformation, of resilience. It's about proving that luxury and elegance don't have to come at the expense of the planet. It's about redefining what 'value' truly means in fashion."

She often spoke of Mrs. Albright, acknowledging her mentor's role in shaping her artistic vision. "Mrs. Albright taught me discipline," Pennelopi would say. "She taught me to listen to the materials, to understand form, to demand integrity from my work. She saw potential when I only saw limitations, and she pushed me to transcend them. She taught me that true art requires not just passion, but rigorous intellectual engagement."

Mrs. Albright, back in their small town, watched Pennelopi's meteoric rise with her characteristic impassive expression, but in the quiet moments, a faint, almost imperceptible smile would touch her lips. She never sought credit, never boasted. She simply observed, a quiet satisfaction in her eyes, knowing she had played a pivotal role in nurturing a truly unique talent.

Pennelopi's personal growth throughout this whirlwind was profound. The crippling shyness, which had once been a defining characteristic, had largely receded. It wasn't that she had become an extrovert overnight; she still cherished her quiet moments, her solitude with her fabrics. But the fear of public scrutiny, the paralyzing anxiety of speaking in front of others, had been replaced by a quiet confidence, a deep well of self-belief born from her achievements and her unwavering artistic integrity. She had learned that her voice, though soft, carried immense power when it spoke of truth and passion.

She found herself standing taller, her posture more assured, a direct application of Mrs. Albright's early instruction: *Do not slouch. Stand tall. Your work deserves it.* Her glasses, once a barrier, now seemed to frame eyes that held a new depth, a quiet wisdom beyond her years.

The future, once an uncertain landscape, now stretched before her, a canvas of endless possibilities. She was already sketching new designs, envisioning her next collection for the main New York Fashion Week runway. She planned to delve deeper into unconventional upcycled materials, exploring industrial waste, forgotten textiles from different cultures, and even collaborating with scientists on innovative sustainable fabric technologies. Her message of conscious consumption and circular fashion would remain at the core of her brand.

She envisioned a future where her brand, "The Upcycled Dream," would not just create beautiful clothes, but would also inspire a global movement towards more sustainable and ethical practices in the fashion industry. She wanted to establish workshops in underserved communities, teaching others the art of upcycling, empowering them to find beauty and economic opportunity in discarded materials. She wanted to prove that true style wasn't about money, but about ingenuity, about passion, about a profound respect for the planet and its resources.

One evening, back in New York, after a particularly exhausting day of interviews and meetings, Pennelopi found herself alone in the quiet Airbnb. She walked over to the makeshift rack where her collection still hung, illuminated by the soft glow of a single lamp. She ran her fingers over the denim of the phoenix dress, the silk of the evening gown, the wool of the sculptural coat. Each piece whispered of its journey, of its transformation, of the hands that had brought it to life.

She thought of her small bedroom back home, filled with fabric mountains. She thought of her parents' sacrifices, Liam's unwavering belief, Mrs. Albright's uncompromising lessons. She thought of the initial dismissal at the local fair, the fear of public speaking, the moments of self-doubt. And she thought of the thunderous applause, the glowing reviews, the title of "youngest designer."

It had been an arduous journey, filled with challenges and triumphs. But every stitch, every struggle, every moment of doubt and every surge of inspiration had led her here. To this moment. To this realization.

Pennelopi Minyen, the shy teen with glasses, had not just become a fashion designer. She had become a voice. A visionary. A star. And she was just getting started. The upcycled dream, once a fragile whisper, now roared with the power of a thousand transformed threads, ready to weave a new future for fashion, one stitch at a time.

www.ingramcontent.com/pod-product-compliance
Ingram Content Group UK Ltd.
Pitfield, Milton Keynes, MK11 3LW, UK
UKHW020141250726
13967UKWH00002B/800

9 781088 051245